HARVEY COX is the Victor S. Thomas Professor of Divinity and chair of the Department of Applied Theology at Harvard's Divinity School. He is widely known for the seminal work *The Secular City* and for a number of other books—including *The Feast of Fools* and *The Seduction of the Spirit*. Long involved with the civil rights, anti-war, and anti-nuclear movements, Cox was one of the first champions of Latin America's liberation theologies. Today, he continues to be at the forefront of the peace movement.

evocative tones, and in a variety of literary modes: a letter to his long-deceased grandmother, an imaginary sequence of memos between two East German military police officers, a reconstructed dialogue between Cox and his son on the glory days of the Civil Rights Movement, and excerpts from various journals and diaries.

Especially memorable is Cox's account of his years as a civil rights activist living in Roxbury, a black ghetto in Boston. His experiences there and his brief hunger strike in jail are rich in humor despite their underlying seriousness. But the focal point of Cox's life and calling—and this book—is most apparent when he asserts that the "highest priority today is to try to prevent our species from joining the brontosaurus and pterodactyl, perhaps taking our lovely, fragile planet along with it."

Cox's disarmingly communicative writing will rivet your attention. Refreshingly *non*-polemical, his carefully reasoned views openly reflect his earnestness and sense of mission. This is one faith journey that will easily reach out to persons across the entire theological and political spectrum.

# Just as I Am

# JOURNEYS IN FAITH

# Just as I Am

## Harvey Cox

Journeys in Faith
Robert A. Raines, Editor

**ABINGDON PRESS**
Nashville

JUST AS I AM

**Library of Congress Cataloging in Publication Data**

COX, HARVEY GALLAGHER.
  Just as I am.
  (Journeys in faith)
  1. Cox, Harvey Gallagher. 2. Theologians—United States—Biogra-
phy. 3. Theology, Doctrinal—United States—History—20th century. I.
Title. II. Series.
BX4827.C68A34        1983        230'.044'0924 [B]        82-11631

**ISBN 0-687-20687-1**

MANUFACTURED BY THE PARTHENON PRESS AT
NASHVILLE, TENNESSEE, UNITED STATES OF AMERICA

*Just as I am, without one plea,*
*But that thy blood was shed for me,*
*And that thou bidst me come to thee,*
*O Lamb of God, I come, I come!*

Hymn text by
Charlotte Elliott

# Contents

# Editor's Foreword

People inside and outside the church today are engaged in a profound revisioning of the faith journey. Wanting to honor our own heritage and to be nourished by our roots we also want to discern the signs of the kingdom now, and to move into the 1980s with a lean, biblical, ecumenical and human faith perspective.

The Journeys in Faith book series is offered to facilitate this revisioning of faith. Reflecting on the social justice openings of the 1960s and the inward searching of the 1970s, these books articulate a fresh integration of the faith journey for the years ahead. They are personal and social. Authors have been invited to share what has been happening to them in their faith and life in recent years, and then to focus on issues that have become primary for them in this time.

We believe that these lucidly written books will be widely

used by study groups in congregations, seminaries, colleges, renewal centers, orders and denominations, as well as for personal study and reflection.

Our distinguished authors embody a diversity of experience and perspective which will provide many points of identification and enrichment for readers. As we enter into the pilgrimages shared in these books we will find resonance, encouragment, and insight for a fresh appropriation of our faith, toward personal and social transformation.

This book tells the story of Harvey Cox just as he is. A Baptist. An irrepressibly curious pilgrim. A traveler to exotic and unlikely places and people. A constant advocate of the oppressed. Cox shares his own family and faith root systems in such a way as to enable his readers to remember and reflect on their own. His faith journey is often triggered toward transformation by a trip. The external journey becomes an inner pilgrimage, and we are in on it and find ourselves reconnecting with our own pilgrimage.

Cox takes us through the "issues" of the last twenty years: the Civil Rights Movement of the sixties, his experience living in a predominantly black section of a city, the Vietnam anguish, the Latin and South American explosions of the Spirit. He takes us with him to the Vatican and to Hiroshima. It is his way to assimilate what is currently happening, allowing that knowledge to deepen and broaden his own humanity and Christianity.

He reflects on his relationship with his father and son. His story is generational and generative and rekindles in us the meanings of our relationships with parents and children. He tells stories and anecdotes, shares letters and conversations, both real and imaginary. He writes in a conversational, colorful, and unpretentious way. He has given us the gift of Harvey Cox, just as he is today. This is a good book for those who want to reflect on their own faith journey through the faith journal of a friend and brother on the pilgrimage.

*Robert A. Raines*

# 1
# Welsh Veins and Quaker Blood

"Overbrook, Merion, Narberth, Wynnewood, Haverford, Bryn Mawr . . . " the conductor's voice intones the familiar stops on the old Pennsylvania Railroad's Paoli local as the train loads passengers at Philadelphia's 30th Street Station. But the sounds are more than stations to me. They are veins, connective tissue running far, far back and far, far away. Like Llanerch, St. Davids, Duffryn Mawr, and Malvern—the town where I was born—these names were all packed into satchels and duffel bags and carried along on sailing vessels by the first Europeans to settle in what is now called Chester County, in the southeast corner of William Penn's woods. They came in the last decades of the seventeenth century, and they brought also the names of the tunes I sang as a boy in the Malvern Baptist Church: Aberystwyth, Hyfrydol, Ffigysbren, Llanfair, Cwm Rhondda. They came from Wales, and they brought their places' names along with them. My life began with these roots all around me. I could hardly avoid them.

My ancestors in Chester County fused by marriage two of the main streams of immigration. The earliest were Quakers.

13

They came from Wales to escape the same religious persecution that had driven an even earlier contingent to leave England. The later ones were Rhineland pietists, German-speaking people who left their homeland rather than be conscripted into the army. Over many decades the two tribes met, argued, traded, visited, courted, married, and raised families. Some prospered; some did not. Some clung to the ancestral faith. Others gradually let it drop. During the era of the great revivals some became Baptists and Methodists. But their family names—Bennet, Bollinger, Dunwoody, Frisch-koln, Hampton—and the names of the places they brought along continued to link succeeding generations with those before.

No one's faith journey begins at birth. It starts eons back with the mothers and fathers of our great-grandmothers and great-grandfathers, and before. Our faith seeps into our corpuscles carried on the songs we hear before we know what their words mean. It enters us with voiceless grimaces, smiles, and distant looks, whispered secrets, tics, smells, stories, all incorporated into our tissue before we are aware of it. It comes to us bound up with caste and class, with color and gender, with language and cuisine. We all meet ourselves, as Søren Kierkegaard once put it, on a ship already launched, a journey already underway.

Malvern, the little town where I grew up, is named for the Malvern Hills near Wales. It is a town with a remarkably inconspicuous history, best known outside its tiny environs today as the site of a Roman Catholic retreat center called St. Joseph's-in-the-Woods, an irony the town's Quaker founders would probably find mildly disquieting. Its one puny claim to historical significance is that on the night of September 20, 1777, a skirmish took place there between some Continental troops under the command of General "Mad Anthony" Wayne and some British soldiers commanded by General Charles Grey. The British apparently surprised the American en-campment at night and the rebels were badly beaten. Some one hundred fifty Americans died, mainly by bayoneting. The

following morning the local farmers gathered at the scene of the
mayhem and buried in a common grave as many bodies as they
could find, erecting a simple stone pyre over the spot. Years later
the pile of stones was replaced by a simple monument and, still
later, by an imposing fifteen-foot polished obelisk.

The "Paoli Massacre" as it came to be called was not an
important battle in any sense. It probably convinced the
members of the Continental Congress, who until then were still
hoping to spend the winter in Philadelphia, the rebel capital, to
move to Trenton. It did cause a fluster of criticism of Anthony
Wayne who was investigated by a court-martial for dereliction
of duty, but unanimously acquitted. Still, it remains a minor
incident familiar only to close students of the Revolutionary
War. For my family, however, it has become a kind of symbol of
where our faith came from and what it means.

In his book *Paoli Massacre,* published in West Chester,
Pennsylvania, in 1877, the hundredth anniversary of the
event, J. S. Futhey includes the following paragraph:

> On the night of the massacre, while the slaughter was going on, the
> family of Joseph Cox, living nearby, were aroused by a man outside
> calling to them. The Battle of Brandywine having occurred but a
> short time before, and the family knowing the soldiers were in the
> neighborhood, had been living in a state of apprehension and
> excitement and were easily awakened. Joseph immediately arose,
> hoisted the window and asked, "who is there?" "For God's sake get
> up, we're all routed," the man replied, "don't you hear them?" At
> this every member of the family was soon at the windows listening
> to the work of carnage. There was born to them distinctly on the
> midnight air, the sounds of the British as they rushed through the
> camp, in their demon-like madness and murderous intent, crying
> out with vociferous yell the Americans' watchword of the night
> "here we are and there they go," and crackling of leaves and bushes
> as men rushed through them, and groans of the wounded as they
> lay where stabbed with swords and bayonets, becoming fainter and
> fainter until they died. (p. 42)

Futhey, whose description of the bloodthirstiness of the
British rings a little oddly in our ears today—since we are

taught that it is Iranians and Russians or Libyans who are bloodthirsty—does not tell us how the family of my ancestors responded to the midnight guest's yelling. It is hard to believe they simply went back to sleep. Such events did not occur very often in the quiet of rural Chester County. They still do not. The account does continue however:

> Early the next morning, a soldier came to the house of Joseph Cox to borrow of him a plain coat and hat to wear back to the place to look after his fallen comrades, saying he was afraid to go in his uniform, lest some of the English might be lying around to kill any American soldiers that might return. (p. 42)

Although Futhey does not go on from here, the oral tradition in my family says that Joseph Cox lent the soldier his coat and that shortly thereafter he and his sons joined their neighbors in digging the huge grave and burying the dead Americans.

### Flashback

He had hardly slept a wink that whole cold and rainy night. Nor had his wife or children. The screams and shouts, but only an occasional gunshot, had pierced the sodden darkness like comets falling. Then there was the soldier who roused them in the middle of the night, and the other one asking for the coat in the morning. Now he told his sons to dress and to bring along picks and spades. Boots pulled on and their broad-brimmed hats deflecting the rain which still fell, lightly now, on the finely tilled farm, they all made their way to where the tents and cooking tripods had stood. There they stopped.

The British general, Grey, had done his work with finesse. He had ordered the attack on the surprised rebels to be made with bayonets alone and had even insisted that his men remove the flints from their locks so there would be no accidental firing to sound the alarm. The killing completed, the British wiped their blades and returned to their encampment near Howell's Tavern at the junction of Bear and Swedesford Roads.

Joseph Cox and his sons stood for several minutes and gazed in silence at the results of the night's activities spread before them. Piles of twisted bodies, all dead by bayonet. The rain falling on the mud washed gulleys of blood into the porous earth. Neighbors arrived. The digging began. By early afternoon the grave was completed. The men placed the bodies, many of them farm boys the same age as the ones doing the digging, side by side. When they had covered them and tamped down the earth all stood quietly, "after the manner of Friends." No prayers were said, no verses read. Quakers believe that the souls of the dead are already with God. More human words would only be redundant. Then, shaking hands with their neighbors, Joseph Cox and his sons returned, picks and shovels on their shoulders, to their farmhouse.

*  *  *  *  *

Although the skirmish took place in what is now called Malvern, it soon became known as the Paoli Massacre because Wayne sent in his dispatch from the Paoli Tavern, a few miles east. The mass grave of the Continental soldiers lies about one-half mile across pastures and cornfields from the home where I grew up one-hundred-sixty years after the event. It was, indeed, a minor battle, scarcely noticed except in the most comprehensive histories. But for Joseph Cox and his family it can hardly have been a minor incident. Nor is it for me. Minor events in world history have a way of becoming major for those most intimately involved and for those who pass on the stories. Joseph Cox was my several-times-great-grandfather. As many years separate him from me as separate me from some descendants of mine who might—if our species survives—live in the 2100s.

Yet I know Joseph Cox in a way. As a boy I used to stand near the mass grave and imagine what he and his sons saw. A few years later, at seventeen, I stood in the shattered debris of Gdansk just after World War II. Still later I stood next to the cold ovens at Auschwitz, then on Seminary Ridge in

Gettysburg, and later still at the simple monument in Hiroshima that marks the epicenter of the first atomic bomb blast. Each time I felt my silent ancestor by my side. I sensed that there is a revulsion against killing and war within me that is so tenacious it could not possibly have started as recently as my own birth. Do I have, as my aunts and uncles who still attended Goshen Meeting when I was a child always told me, "Quaker blood"?

I suppose I do. But who *were* they, these fiercely faithful men and women who while still in England had their fingers cut off for refusing to doff their hats to the king, who when they came to Massachusetts were stripped and whipped on the backs of carts from Boston to Salem and banished into the blizzards? What gave them their towering audacity, their rage against pretense and plumage, their exasperating insistence on speaking the truth however inconvenient, their taste for simplicity and inner serenity? What led them to their refusal to bear arms for anyone?

They are mostly gone now, this breed of Quaker. Parts of their tradition remain—in the quiet of the silent meeting, the peace vigils, the risky service to unpopular causes. But I often wish I could have met some of the originals, the ones who had been hounded from England to Wales and then chased to Penn's Woods: my forebears. They must have been tough and tender, formidable, and yet somehow attractive. To understand them might help me understand the strange something that binds me to the sod behind the Goshen Meeting House and the stark old cemeteries and family plots of Chester County: my Quaker blood.

Today I live five-hundred miles from Tredyffrin and Goshen and Malvern, in the smug city that once lashed Quakers and banished Baptists. But, though I have dwelt in the Boston area for twenty years, something still seems severed. A part of me belongs near that weedy mound with its somber stone monument, the inscription nearly effaced by two centuries of rain. In my faith journey I have to go back, time and again, and stand there with Joseph Cox and his sons on the day that surely was the most memorable they ever lived. Through some strange time warp, some mystery of transubstantiated history, that day is also a day in *my* history. I was there.

# 2
# On Starting a Book

I am glad this book is underway. Starting anything, especially something new is never easy for me. There is a cautious dybbuk curled-up inside my skull that craves the familiar, the time-tested. Yet any journey requires us to leave somewhere, to start off for somewhere else; and, we are never sure what the "else" will turn out to be. So we linger, cling, even loiter. We procrastinate, or at least I do, a lot. Yet the metaphor of journey is at the center of our faith and—when I think about it—at the center of human life as well. Like trying to avoid decisions, trying to avoid the journey never works. "Not to decide," I once wrote in a book long ago, "is to decide." Choices get made *for* us whether we like it or not; so it is always better to make them as best we can, to exercise our God-bestowed gift of decision making. Otherwise we forfeit the most valuable capacity the Creator has given us. Even love, after all, is not just a sentiment. It is a matter of deciding to love.

So it is with journeying. Life does not allow us to stand still. Things change, around us and within us. Parents get old and die. Children grow up and leave. Friends and co-workers move away and move on. Our own legs and eyes and backs remind us in daily irrefutable ways that we are not the men and women we once were.

As one who has lived most of my life in an academic community where generations of students come and go so relentlessly, I am slapped in the face every spring by the irresistible transiency of life. Caps and gowns always make me sniffle. I also know, however, that such a community is only a more graphic example of the primal fact of human transiency. Like Goethe's Faust I have often wanted to say, "Verweile euch!" Wait awhile! Don't move so fast! But, though we may loiter, life does not. With or without our compliance the journey limps on. New faces and new situations intrude and upset us, and sometimes gladden us despite our preference for what has been. Not to decide is to decide, and "not to journey is to journey anyway"; so in the long run it is better to be a purposeful traveler, choosing our routes as much as we can, than to be a hog-tied hostage dragged along by forces we cannot influence.

I said "influence," not control. The distinction is important. As I have grown older I have become more suspicious of the pressing need I once felt to be in control of my own destiny. Such compulsion, I have come to believe, is only the other side of the resignation and fatalism I also reject. It may be the principal cause of "burn-out." The old "serenity prayer" asks not only for the "serenity to accept the things I cannot change," and "the courage to change the things I can," but also, and maybe most important, for "the wisdom to know the difference." It is that wisdom which is for me the mark of maturity. People who have it keep going. It is the compulsives who burn out.

All this may sound surprising at first coming from the pen of one who has thought of himself, and been seen by others, as a changer and influencer, even perhaps as an "activist" (whatever that is). I see no contradiction. What I have learned, often painfully, is that I can only influence and change things—whether in my own life or in the larger world—when I first recognize and accept the things I *cannot* change. Such acceptance is the opposite of fatalism. It liberates me to focus my energies on the things that *can* be changed.

Maybe this has to do with the *vita activa* and the *vita contemplativa*. They have been wrenched asunder so relentlessly in most of Western religious history. "Some pray, others work," it was said, and even the Reformation did not heal the fissure. But the two are not, I am convinced, alternative modes of life. They are essential ingredients in any mature person. The people I have admired most in life are a mixture of the two. That may be why, to the puzzlement of some of my faculty colleagues, I offer courses both on liberation theology and social ethics on the one hand and on contemplative and spiritual disciplines on the other. These seemingly diverse interests reveal my own yearning for that fitting combination of contemplation and action which alone blossoms in the "wisdom" of the "Serenity Prayer."

So I have now started a book on my faith journey and like any book or any journey, the hardest part is the beginning. A thousand questions scratch at the windows and crawl under the door. How can I write about a journey that has been so erratic and directionless, that keeps circling back to a barren meadow in Pennsylvania, to scenes already played? How can I be honest not only about the milestones I have passed, the people, events, and ideas that have touched me but also about the pain and the failure? Why would anyone want to read about anyone else's faith journey anyway?

The only satisfactory answer I can give to these questions is to think of this book as itself a part of the journey it recalls. I see it as an opportunity to hum the old songs again, to listen to the scratchy tapes, to look at the browning, dog-eared photos, to examine with as much candor as I can muster, some past steps of my faith journey in the hope that doing so will help me exorcise the dybbuk and take the next step.

One feature of this account the reader will notice immediately is that its style is inconsistent and even discordant. The chapters are of uneven length. Some pages are in straightforward narrative; others are real or imaginary interviews; letters never sent; reconstructed and partially fabricated conversations; journal entries; elements of apologia; confession and—I am sure—a little dissimulation. The hodgepodge character of the book is intentional. Style and form are always a part of the message. My faith journey has not been a continuous one or a steady climb up the ladder of "faith development." It has been desultory and meandering. There have been sickening reversals and absurd contradictions. There have been times in my life when I have lived more in the past than in the present, when memories of events gone by have seemed more vivid than what was happening under my nose. There have been detours and dead ends. Sometimes my journey takes me past the same landmarks several different times. I want the pastiche patchwork of the book to say something about the journey itself.

### A Miniature Flashback

It is September 1978. My knees shaking, I am standing in my green shorts, orange T-shirt and blue-and-yellow Brooks running shoes along with some two hundred other fidgety would-be runners at the starting line of the Chilmark five-kilometer road race on Martha's Vineyard. At forty-nine it is my first race. I had started running, along with Jim Fixx and millions of other middle-aged Americans only a few months before. My stomach is knotted and my throat is tight. I have no hope of winning of course, not even in my age class. What I do want to do is finish, and if possible, not be the last across the line.

Waiting for the starting signal seems endless. Eventually the Chilmark police officer fires his pistol. I grunt and lumber the five kilometers. With cardiovascular muscles pounding and lungs pumping I finish (not last). My wife and children meet me at the finish with an apple, some fresh cookies, and some cold lemonade. I feel depleted, but great.

* * * * *

When I think about that race today what I remember most is not the end, not the ferocious hills or the aching thighs. I remember the start. I was beginning something. I felt awkward and inept, afraid I could be humiliated, unsure if I would finish. Yet I also sensed a strange exhilaration: to start something new puts us in a special relation to the One who says, "Behold, I make all things new."

I begin this book with many of the same hestitations. Sure, I have written books before, maybe too many of them. Still, I have never written this one. I feel just as awkward and unsure as I did that day in Chilmark, but also equally exhilarated. I have no desire to win, only to run the whole way and to finish; and even if friends and family are there with a cooling drink when I write the last sentence, it will be this beginning I will remember most clearly, this moment in this untidy office. There is nothing quite like starting something new.

# 3
# Letter to a Terrific Old Lady, Long Since Dead

*Thanksgiving Day 1981*

Dear Maude,

I know I never called you "Maude" when you were alive, although nearly everyone else did. I always called you "Grandma," and when you died in 1952, I hid in the attic among the Christmas tree decorations and faded lampshades so I could sob where no one would hear me. I loved you, and you were the first "significant other" (a present psychologistic circumlocution you would not have liked) to die on me. I am writing to you now, thirty years later, because you, like most of the people most of us love, died before I could tell you how much I loved you. Also, you were one terrific old lady, and—although I have my doubts about the occult, seances, and communicating with people in your present location—I do hope that somehow this letter reaches you.

"My grandmother!" What a wagonload of trite associations: a prim, crackly little voice; rimless glasses over the nose; patiently knitted sweaters; gentle old-fashioned advice to Mom on how to mix the mincemeat. Thank God, Maude, you were nothing like that. You dressed, to put it in a kind word,

nonchalantly. Your slip often sagged beneath your off-the-
rack print dresses. Your laughter sometimes embarrassed
people because it was loud, ended in a long diminishing sigh,
and came often. You were a casual housekeeper and I never
saw you so much as hold a knitting needle. As far as giving my
mother any advice in the kitchen, everyone knew you were a
slapdash cook—at least around your own house, although you
loved to join the other women in mixing huge gleaming vats of
potato salad or cole slaw for the Firemen's Fair or the Sunday
school picnic. I strongly suspect it was the talk and not the food
preparation that drew you to these culinary scenes. Peeling
and baking and broiling at home were no fun for you because
you had to be alone, and that you pointedly did not like. My
grandfather, your husband (may he also rest in peace)
subsisted for years on the deftly recycled surpluses of the most
recent church basement supper. If he ever complained, I
never heard it.

How did you influence my faith journey, Maude? By
teaching me to say the Lord's Prayer or instilling respect for the
clergy? Hardly. Although you almost never missed a Sunday at
our little Baptist church and I sat next to you in the pew, you
always sat a little sidewise, finding who else was in church and
how they looked more interesting than what was coming from
the choir or the pulpit. As far as the clergy went, although you
never really actively *dis*liked our ministers, you seemed to view
them as a sort of necessary evil. They came and went, staying
two or three years until they were called to "wider fields of
service." With them came and went their particular theological
emphases and personal eccentricities. Some favored revivals,
some did not. One approved of using the basement for church
suppers, the next one did not. The church itself, however,
went on. And on and on. Thinking back, it seems to me you
knew even then, Maude, without reading my books on "the
theology of the laity," that you and the people like you *were* the
church. Also (using another term you would have found a little
pretentious), as a part of what Catholics call the "church
triumphant," you still *are* the church. I hope you find the music

there more in tune and the crowd as worth sizing up as you did at our church.

How did you do it, Maude? How, splattered week after week with such uneven and inconsistent preaching, instructed in Sunday school in such an amateur way, did you turn out to be just what everyone says we need today, a "Christian politician"? Because that's what you were. Politics was your passion. Not big international issues but local, county, and sometimes state politics, and, every four years, presidential elections. You were not, as I recall, particularly ideological. You worked in the Republican Party. But you worked in it more, I suspect, because that was about all there was in small-town eastern Pennsylvania in those days. If you had lived in Alabama you would have been a Democrat and if you had lived in the USSR you would probably have belonged to the local Communist party organization. Like mixing the cole slaw, you wanted to be where the action was, where the excitement, the influence, the decision making seemed to be going on. You lapped it up.

You were, Maude, on numberless committees, part of a vast web of connections that seemed to be wired into your standing tubular telephone with the separate earpiece (like the ones the new gentry buy today in urban boutiques). And your networks got me, your first grandchild, to some fabulous places. Now at last I can thank you as I never did before for taking me with you to that "Alfred Landon for President" picnic at Rustic Park in 1936; to the state Republican convention when it met in Philadelphia at the Bellevue Stratford and you were an elected delegate; to the election night party in 1940 when your candidate, Wendell Wilkie, lost to FDR and some people cried, but you did not. Why cry? It had been an exciting campaign, lots of phone calls, and besides by then you were growing accustomed to losing presidential elections to "that man. . . . " Also, you had delivered your precinct, and it was not going to change things in our town very much anyway, or so you thought. It seemed as though nothing ever changed our town. After the election you philosophically gave me a wooden cigar box full of Wendell Wilkie campaign buttons, which I still have in my desk drawer. They are probably worth a lot of money to antiquarians today like copies of *Action Comics* and baseball cards. But don't worry, Maude, I'll never sell them. Never.

But, my overtrained theological mind presses: were you really a *Christian* politician? What connections, an inquirer would ask, did you make between your faith and your politics? Again, I think the question would have puzzled you. Your name, after all, was Hampton, an old Virginia name. Your father had come to Pennsylvania from Virginia as a horse trader. Somewhere there is an old photograph of you as a young woman of about twenty seated confidently astride one of his bay mares. (You were the village beauty—blond, blue-eyed, five feet ten. No one could ever explain why you married my diminutive and somewhat prissy grandfather. Maybe to avoid having anyone get in your way?) In any case, as a Hampton from Virginia, being a Baptist for you was not something you particularly had to *choose* to be. Virginia was teeming with Baptists. Still, as a Baptist in our county, where by that time the Quakers had become an old family aristocracy, your father, and therefore you too must have been viewed at first as parvenus.

You distinctly disliked pretense, snootiness, and people who thought just having money brought with it any kind of virtue. You were on such friendly terms with the black people in our town some white folks viewed it as scandalous. You were the one who first took me to visit the A.M.E. church. Also, you never made the judgments other people made on the drunks, riffraff, ne'er-do-wells, and idlers of the community. Although you probably did not know the meaning of the term *populist,* you had a hearty disdain for big business, party bosses, rich people, and any government organ from the county court-house to the White House that seemed to be run by anyone you could not ring up on your tubular telephone. You thought of yourself as being on the side of the ordinary people who have to work for a living, sometimes lose their jobs and fall into hard luck, occasionally get drunk and maybe not go to church, but are better people by far than the ones who look down on them from their places of power.

Did that make you a Christian politician? I make no judgments. Some liberation theologies today would no doubt applaud your "identification with the poor" or even your incipient class consciousness. But they would be awfully puzzled by those Wilkie buttons.

I remember, Maude, the hot July day I went to church and you were not in your customary pew. I fidgeted through the hymns and prayers and sermon wondering where you were, then dashed out right after the benediction to look for you. My parents told me the news. The doctor had put you to bed. You had a pain in the middle of your chest that even you could not ignore. You were seventy-three. He told you to lie still for five weeks. You did not, of course. Within a few days you were up, telephoning, keeping the network buzzing, ordering the wieners for the fair, receiving friends in your unkempt living room. A week later you were dead.

I could not believe it when they told me. Some people in the family sniffled. Others kept a stiff upper lip. My father was your only child and I was his firstborn. So I was a grandchild to you in a way none of my brothers or sisters ever quite was. You sneaked me off to gather shellbarks and bluebells and to buy cider and homemade ice cream at the outlying farms. You sang me the ballad about "Morgan the Raider" to put me to sleep at naptime. (How, come to think of it, did you ever find the time to do that?) So when they told me, I climbed to the attic, closed the door, and sat among the sad, dusty ornaments. Ever since that day I have wanted to say all this and now, as I write about my "faith journey," I have a chance at last. I'm glad I do.

So Maude, it is time to end this rambling letter. Oh, I know you are in no hurry. Where you are, ten thousand years is but as an afternoon. Anyway, even down here you never tired of a conversation with anyone. Supper could burn to a cinder while you laughed and gossiped on the phone. I hope heaven has at least a few residents who suffer from arthritis or piles or cramps so you can inquire about their health and listen while they rattle on. I hope it also has an occasional kid who has gotten into a little trouble with the law and needs a friendly call to the justice of the peace. I hope it has Firemen's Fairs with sauerkraut, cottage cheese, and hot dogs for sale. Otherwise, Maude, I'm afraid you might find the Beulah Land we sang about in church a little boring. On the other hand, even if the manna is "in bountiful supply," the sky is always cloudless and the fountain "never shall run dry," you will—I'm sure—*never* get bored. You will find *something* that needs doing or needs improving. You will find a phone and, with an eternity to work on it, think of all the fun you will have.

Love,
Harvey

# 4
# The Voyage of the
# *Robert Hart*

In 1946, when I was seventeen, like nearly every seventeen-year-old I have ever known (including three of my own) I wanted to get AWAY. I was a high school student during the Second World War. I watched older friends and cousins disappear from town and return after basic training in blue or khaki uniforms. I watched some of them leave and not come back again, ever. Despite my Quaker roots, along with everyone else in Malvern, I was caught up in the "Win-the-war-against-the-Germans-and-the-Japs" enthusiasm of the last popular war America fought. But in a secret place in my heart I did *not* want the war to be over, not until I had been in it.

It did end, however, in 1945, with two mushroom clouds over Hiroshima and Nagasaki. With my high school friends I celebrated V.E. Day and V.J. Day by blowing noisemakers and riding around on fire engines with the sirens screaming. But inwardly I was crestfallen. History had, it seemed, passed me by.

But not completely. The following spring, when I was still a junior in high school, I read that the United Nations Relief and

Rehabilitation Administration was shipping livestock to Europe to replenish the devastated herds and that young men were needed on the cattle boats. Still inebriated with adolescent wanderlust and the residue of the going-into-the-service elan, I decided to sign up. I announced my intention to my parents and, to my astonishment, they agreed. Looking back, I am still astonished. Maybe their reluctance was lessened by the fact that the Church of the Brethren Service committee, which had carried on a private project of sending heifers to war-ravaged Europe had been commissioned by UNRRA to recruit and train the seagoing cowboys. In any case, within a few weeks, just after the last day of classes in 1946 I arrived in Baltimore, Maryland, to ship out on an antiquated, rusting Liberty ship called the *Robert Hart* with a cargo of foaled mares and cows. Our destination was Gdansk, Poland, known more recently for the historic strike in the Lenin shipyard and the beginning of the Solidarity movement in Poland.

Herman Melville has written somewhere that the ship he first sailed on was his "Yale and Harvard." Although I later attended both those institutions, I know what he meant. I learned more and grew up more during those weeks on the *Robert Hart* than during any other period of my life. The faculty of Robert Hart University consisted of the ship's crew and officers, my fellow "cowboys," and especially the "supervisor," the martinet who was in charge of the cowboy crew. A diminutive Simon Legree with a colossal ego and a rasping foghorn bass voice, he obviously knew what we greenhorns whispered to one another in our minuscule sleeping quarters on the ship's fantail: that in the pantheon of the *Robert Hart,* the captain was God Almighty and he was Jesus Christ. My image of Jesus, nurtured by Sallman's *Head of Christ* and pictures in Sunday school books, was a different one. Still, he was a man I decided not to cross if I could possibly avoid it. I knew I was at his mercy and that his idea of mercy was not that of gentle Jesus meek and mild.

Maybe I tried a little too hard. In any case one day, about a thousand miles out of Baltimore, he saw me trying to slip by him unnoticed. He stopped me and ordered me to descend to the lower 'tween deck and to hold onto the end of a bulky hawser, the other end of which was being used to hoist a canvas ventilator to siphon fresh air down to the horses. He told me to hold onto it with all my might, insinuating that I did not have much, while he supervised the rigging. He warned me not to let go of it or climb back out until he told me to.

I obeyed. Although I was supposed to be watering the horses on another deck at the time and had been on my way to that assignment, something told me that if I had not said, "Yes, sir!" I could expect anything from the cat-o-nine-tails to keelhauling. I had probably read too many sea stories. Jack London's *Sea Wolf* and Richard Henry Dana's *Two Years Before the Mast* had been my favorites as a fourteen-year-old. Up until then the supervisor had not seemed to notice me, and I had considered myself lucky, but now he had issued a direct command. I climbed down the ladder with the rope and, so as not to be pulled into the hatch opening by the tugging I could feel from above, planted myself a few yards back in a position where I could not see out and braced myself against a girder.

I had seen canvas ventilators hoisted before and I knew the whole operation took only about five minutes. Although the pressure on my arms felt like it was pulling them out of the sockets I was determined (a) to prove to the supervisor that I was not the weakling he implied I was, and (b) not do or fail to do anything that would arouse his ire. Ten minutes passed, then fifteen, then twenty. My arms and neck and back ached, but every time I eased my weight on the hawser it began slipping up, dragged by the force of the stiff north Atlantic winds. When my watch showed that a half hour had passed I began to panic. I could not hold on much longer. What to do? If I let go, I imagined the vent flying off the rigging into the ocean. If I tied the hawser around my waist and climbed back out I would have disobeyed the deity. Frantic, I looked at the horses who munched nonchalantly on their hay and offered no advice or succor. I began to wonder why I had not stayed in Malvern and taken that job in Aunt Mary's drugstore. I also began to understand what it might have felt like when the inquisitors stretched Joan of Arc on the rack.

Finally I could take it no longer. Tying the hawser around my waist as best I could I tried to climb up the steel ladder only to find that my arms were too exhausted to cling to the rungs. Slowly and laboriously I made my way up, throwing my whole arm over each step so I would not drop three decks, the hawser still around my waist. After ten minutes of agonized ascent I crawled onto the deck. The supervisor was nowhere in sight. The line had been looped over a crane and the ventilator lay folded on the deck. I had been tricked. Humiliated. And not by one of my fellow cowboys, but by a man who had the legitimate authority to tell me what to do.

Now the inner pain began to exceed the aches in my arms. I quickly made my way to my own hold and started watering the horses with my mates who asked me in less-than-friendly tones where the hell I had been. I avoided their eyes and mumbled that I had been "doing a job for the supervisor." When I saw the little despot later in the day he glanced at me slyly but I did not ask him what happened. I had had enough abasement for one day.

That night I lay on my bunk unable to sleep because of the pains in my arms and the rage that wracked my stomach and chest. Occasionally I would nod off only to wake up in a minute or two with my shoulders screaming and my saliva turned to acid. For the first time in my life I savored the taste of pure loathing. I *hated* the supervisor. I wanted to kill him, smash his head in with one of the pitchforks, kick him down an open hatch cover, watch him die in piles of reeking manure. What troubled me most, as I winced and tossed was that this petty pasha had *legitimate* authority over me. He *was* my boss. Although I was sure there were some legal limits on what he could do to me, I also knew that in the midst of the ocean there was no one around (except maybe God the captain who dwelt in his own celestial realm and had other things to do) to supervise the supervisor. I could go nowhere to get away from him. That thought stopped my breathing for a moment. No where to go. No court of appeal. I was stuck on a ship with a tyrant whose power over me was not only arbitrary but in some crazy way also legitimate.

I did not lead a mutiny against the supervisor. I chose the coward's path—avoidance, deference, waiting it out. If I saw him on the port side, I would cross to the starboard. I kept out of his range. But ever since that day I carry—in a way that only pain and humiliation can teach—a recognition of why people rebel against tyrants, even those with a legitimate claim to authority. It was not just that single incident with the supervisor and the ventilator line that gave me a feeling for the underdog, the person being cheated, misused, debased. That prejudice probably came to me from many sources. But the will to fight back against domination needs the energy of anger to keep it alive, and often when I imagine myself in the place of any oppressed person anywhere and try to sense what is sustaining them, I remember the supervisor and feel the stitch in my shoulders. Then I know. There is not only "that of God" in every person, there is also that which can only take so much before it fights back. And that too, I believe is of God. In any case, whoever else he was, I decided that night as the *Robert Hart* plowed toward Europe, that the supervisor definitely was *not* Jesus Christ.

If the faculty of Robert Hart University was the crew, its laboratory was the horses and cows. My deck had horses. Foaled mares, bred just before our departure presumably to double the delivery load, they were touchy and irritable. Being stuck in a dark hold for three weeks, never exercised, tossed by the motion of the ship, they constantly stomped and whinnied. Nearly a hundred of the eight hundred we started with died before we reached Europe. Each day we hoisted the dead horses out of the hold with cranes and dropped them into the sea and sharks tore them up as soon as they hit the water.

The horses were not in a good mood and their mood got worse by the day. Two weeks out of Baltimore (remember this was the *Robert Hart,* not the *Queen Mary;* she made eleven knots at full speed) a particularly nervous black mare reached out

and bit me on my left shoulder, still sore from the
time-of-testing with the Antichrist. The bite punctured and
lacerated the skin and I had to be treated by the ship's purser,
the only medical aide on board, whose skills were limited to
aspirin, tincture of iodine, and Scotch. He did not know much
about stitching people up so I was repaired with gauze and
adhesive tape. Thirty-five years later I still carry a tiny stigmata
from that bite. Every time I shower or swim I have a chance to
remember the *Robert Hart,* the black mare, the supervisor.

But it was all worth it. Everyday at sea I leaped out of bed
when the bell rang at five; I was thousands of miles from
Malvern; I was doing something important; I was becoming an
adult. Everyday I made a short entry in a log, still imagining at
times that I was Richard Henry Dana in the days of the clipper
ships. I keep that log in my closet, and when I feel nostalgic
after a dull faculty meeting, I thumb through it. Reading it
always brings back sights and smells. For example, on July 13,
1946, while we were making our way through the North Sea
where leftover mines were still bobbing around I made the
following entry:

> The captain didn't make an inspection today having been awake all
> night taking us through the mine fields. Passed two floating mines
> on the portside about 7:00 P.M. only 50 yards away, a little too close.
> We put empty feed bags soaked in DDT around the hold since the
> flies are really bad. Slept with my life jacket at the foot of my bed.

The words sound flat and reportorial when I read them
today. I don't sound scared. Was I? In those days, a year after
the war, ships still ran into mines that had broken from their
moorings and were floating loose. I'm sure I knew even then
that the *Robert Hart* was not invincible and that I could die at
seventeen, which was not in my life plan. But was I frightened?
Did I pray? I don't think so. I considered myself a Christian,
having been baptized a few years earlier at our local Baptist
church. I remember taking a Bible with me in my blue
seaman's bag. But in 1946 I still must have had that innocent,

late-adolescent omnipotence we float on at seventeen. If the ship itself was not invincible, I somehow assumed *I was*. If it were blown out of the water, I would swim courageously in my life jacket until a rescue vessel came. Then, face coated with oil, like the courageous merchant seamen in the war movies I had seen, I would be hauled aboard, given hot coffee, wrapped in blankets, photographed by the newspapers. Later I would come home with stories that matched anything the war veterans (those who actually came home) told. At seventeen, for me, death was something that happened to other people. I think this is true for most seventeen-year-olds. Maybe that is why the military likes to recruit "teenagers." Millions of them have died in older men's wars over the centuries, probably believing until the last moment that they were indestructible.

The ship did not sink. On a warm July day in 1946 it crept into Novyport, the harbor area of Gdansk. That evening we were given shore passes and I spent the next four hours walking the dim streets with two shipmates. For blocks in every direction Gdansk was rubble. It smelled of rotting garbage and acrid smoke. The proud Hanseatic port and "free city" of Danzig before the war, celebrated more recently by Günter Grass in his novel *The Tin Drum,* had been bombed and shelled by both sides. Bands of children, grime worn into their faces and arms, many wearing the jagged remains of adult castoff clothes, followed us everywhere we went asking for candy, money, and cigarettes. Oily pimps sidled up to us with offers of "my sister" or "my daughter," whistling the way they had heard sailors do at women, describing the voluptuous shape of their ladies-for-sale with hand motions and gestures.

I felt sick and returned to the ship early. Was this the Europe I had looked forward to seeing? Charred wreckage, hungry children, sadness and chaos? The next morning, when my friends wanted to go ashore again, I pretended to be ill. I think I told them I "had a hangover," which always passed as a manlier alibi. I lay in my mattress and stared at the bottom of the bunk above me. So, this was the world outside Malvern, the historic Europe of cathedrals and boulevards and museums I had heard about. Of course I had seen pictures of war rubble. I suppose I knew I would see some. But *this*? Suddenly I wanted to be home again. I wanted to sit on the porch with my father in the twilight while he smoked his pipe and talked about his work, what was happening in town, county politics. I thought of my own little sister, who was then ten, out on the streets at midnight begging for chocolate bars, or being offered for a night of "fucky, fucky" for five dollars. I felt tears welling up but I could not cry. I only clenched my teeth, and for the first time in my life, sensed a cold anger at any God who would let something like this happen.

Later in the day I got hungry and pulled myself out of bed to go to the ship's galley. No one was there, so I opened the big crew refrigerator and made a spam and cheese sandwich. I poured a cup of coffee. But I could not eat. Feeling miserable and lonely I wandered out on deck. The horses and cows were being unloaded by Polish stevedores using flying stalls rigged on the ship's cranes. I sat on a hatch cover and watched.

A few minutes later a Polish dockworker who seemed to be in charge asked me for a cigarette. I gave him a whole pack. He did not light one (they never did—the cigarettes were for the black market) but instead signaled his men to take a break and sat down near me. He spoke a little English, asked me where I was from, how old I was, what I thought of Gdansk.

When I obviously could not answer the last question he said, "Too bad you could not have seen this"—gesturing toward the miles of twisted metal frames and shattered brick—"before the war." I listened. He reminded me of my father somehow. He talked about Danzig in the days before the Nazis, then the Russians, had come. He told me about his home, now destroyed, his family, now nearly all dead, the evening band concerts, the school he had attended. All "before the war."

The war. The war. Slowly I began to realize something. The war I had seen from the secure perspective of high school, and had secretly hoped would last long enough so that I could be in it, had done all this to Gdansk, to him, to the thin children in their oversize, discarded battle jackets and lacerated sweaters.

During the next days, as the ship remained tied up in port and I began to venture back down the gangway and into the town, I sensed a new object for my disgust and revulsion: the war. The war had done this. Of course it had been the Germans and the Russians who had actually fired the cannons and dropped the bombs. I knew that. But something clicked. Had the people who had started, fought, won, lost the war ever considered that it would transform little children the age of my sister into packs of thieving scavengers roaming the alleys? Somehow I did not think about the millions of dead, the incalculable property damage, all the other horrendous costs. I was obsessed with the children. I knew not only that the supervisor was not Jesus Christ but that if there was any God at all, anywhere in the universe, *that* God could not have wanted this to happen.

The voyage home was uneventful. Without the horses and cows to feed there was little for the cowboy crew to do after we had shoveled tons of manure into cargo nets and dumped it into the North Atlantic. I slept in the sun on the hatch cover, read, and thought. I thought a lot. I could not get the memory of those knobby-kneed Polish children out of my mind. As the long, empty days passed, I became aware of a conviction growing inside me that there could not be another war. It just was not worth it.

The voyage of the *Robert Hart* took place many years ago. Like Melville, however, I can say that antiquated old vessel was "my Yale and Harvard." More. It took me to a place where, even without a shot being fired at me, I found out something about who I was and what my life was meant to be. Decades later, standing on the steps of the chapel at the U.S. Air Force Academy in Colorado with Sister Mary Luke Tobin, a group of novice nuns from the religious order she headed, and a small group of church people from Denver, I thought momentarily about that voyage. We were handing out copies of St. Francis' prayer for peace to the Air Force cadets as they entered the chapel for Sunday worship. We were also giving them the latest reports on the current bombing of Vietnam and asking them to think and pray about what they were being trained to do. The security police of the academy first asked us politely to stop it, then ordered us sternly to leave. But this order, unlike the hawser-holding order I had heard from the supervisor, I quietly disobeyed. So did all the nuns. A few minutes later a military police van appeared. We all knelt in prayer on the steps. One by one we were escorted to the van and then to the base prison.

We were only detained for a few hours. Then the air police drove us to the base exit with a personal letter from the commander forbidding us ever to enter the academy grounds again. While we were locked up, however, we talked with one another about where we had first picked up our common revulsion for war, and I heard myself talking about the *Robert Hart*, the streets of Gdansk, the children. I noticed, to my surprise, that I could still remember some of their faces. My voice broke as I spoke, and I even found a New Testament text coming to mind. It was one I had at times thought unduly harsh but in this case seemed appropriate beyond measure: "If anyone should harm one of these little ones, let a millstone be tied about his neck and let him be cast into the midst of the sea" (paraphrased). Yes, into the *sea,* with the dead horses, the sharks, the manure, I thought silently, knowing that the sisters would not appreciate the connection that existed in my mind.

I am sure the *Robert Hart* was sold for scrap soon after the voyage to Gdansk. Liberty ships had been constructed to make only two or three voyages and it had already made several. But I still have a photograph of the *Robert Hart* taken as our motor launch sped away from it when we disembarked the last time in Baltimore. I am fonder of that picture than of those I have of the college buildings I studied in, some of them ivy-covered and venerable.

Recently I began to wonder what happened to those children. Did they survive the hunger and cold of the following winter in Gdansk? Did any of them grow up to become workers in the Lenin shipyards? Was one of them Lech Walesa or one of his associates? I will never know. What I do know is that one travel-entranced American teen-ager was never the same again after his voyage to Gdansk. A youthful adventure, sparked by adolescent restiveness, the reading of sea yarns, and a romantic lust for travel, had unexpectedly become a faith journey. There would be more.

# 5
# Faith of My Father

My father never knew what hit him. His little business went under when he was forty and I was eleven. He was not the same after that. He died fifteen years later still shaking his head about what happened, wondering what he had done wrong.

Like many people of Welsh blood my father was a short, rotund man, generally easygoing but given to occasional dark moods and temper outbursts. After flirting with becoming a pharmacist he had eventually given in to family pressures and taken over from his father a small painting and wallpaper hanging business a few years before I was born. My grandfather had started the business himself after leaving school at the age of nine and serving as an apprentice. Although the name of the firm was impressive—"John Foreman Cox and Son," it read on the little white cards he kept to give out to potential customers—it was not much of a business at all. Never more than four or five men were employed at any one time, usually fewer, and my father worked along with them dressed in a spotted cap and baggy white overalls—like the ones that have recently become fashionable for affluent young women to wear. He stored the paint, ladders, and brushes in our garage and seemed to take more pleasure in mixing and applying the smooth white Dutch Boy to walls and fences than he did from the nagging administrative part of his job: hunting out customers and collecting bills.

Still, even during the Great Depression, there were usually enough barns and houses that needed painting; so we always had food on the table and even owned one half of a brick-and-frame double house. There was no way he could have known that it just could not last.

I was never allowed to play around the paint but I couldn't help smelling it, and even today the odor of turpentine, like the taste of Proust's little Madeline cookie, brings back a whole *temps perdu*. It recalls the times I was allowed to go to work with my father, riding with some of the painters in the back of his covered pickup truck, to some country estate where he was working at the time. He seemed to be an expert, or so I thought, in painting the miles of white fences that crisscrossed the rural section of eastern Pennsylvania near the small town where we lived, the fences of the gentry in the Radnor Hunt Club who rode after foxes and were always referred to by our family as the "horse people."

My family's attitude toward the "horse people" was my first lesson in class consciousness. Class attitudes and animosities are rarely conveyed explicitly. No one in my family ever told me they disliked the horse people. Sometimes, riding through the countryside with visiting relatives, they even pointed out their graceful old houses and barns, especially the ones my father and his men had painted, and stopped to admire the groomed and flawless horses that gazed at us over those gleaming white rails.

But just below the surface of admiration even a child could sense the resentment and the contempt. It was all in the tone of voice: my people did not like the horse people. We had to be nice to them of course. Not obsequious, but pleasant; and they usually made it easy, on those rare occasions when direct interaction was required, by being nice—or at least civil—to us. Still I knew "we" were not like "them." *We* had to work and scrimp and save while *they* had piles of money they hardly knew what to do with. We had to pay a dime for a measly pony ride at the Fire Company Fair, further humiliated by the fact that some kid led the pony by the bridle while we rode. *They* had stables full of glorious horses who all looked like the Lone Ranger's or at least Gene Autry's, and they could leap on them and ride off in crimson jackets and glistening black boots anytime they felt like it. Furthermore, there were always whispered allusions about the antinomian excesses and flamboyant shenanigans of the horse people. They got noisily drunk at their huge parties; they smashed up their convertibles careening over country roads and didn't care how much it cost to fix them; they neglected to oil, varnish, clean, repair or adjust things the way we always had to; so their clocks, stoves, refrigerators and lawn mowers were always being prematurely discarded and new ones bought. But they didn't care. They could pay, and they didn't give a damn. They flitted all over the country, had bizarre tastes in food and decor (which however they could afford to indulge), and seemed to inhabit a world in which the normal proprieties and modulations simply did not apply. In short, they had money. So went the talk, and so I learned about class.

It was not that my family's circle of relatives and friends disapproved of the horse people. That was not the question somehow. Their escapades were never reported in moralistic or judgmental tones; rather they were discussed with a chuckle or an indulgent shake of the head, the way one might describe the exploits of small children. No one organized raiding parties on their estates, fired their houses or slit their horses' throats. The suggestion, ever so subtly conveyed, was not that they were morally corrupt or the perpetrators of injustice, but that they were lucky, not as smart as they wanted to appear, amusing to observe, and above all powerful and therefore people to stay on the right side of. They not only had money, they had connections.

My father rarely joined the sly gossip about the horse people. When it started he would yawn, elaborately empty, load, tamp, and light one of his pipes—or stare out a window, or subtly change the subject. I never knew then why he didn't enjoy that kind of spicy conversation, but more recently I think I know. It wasn't that he liked the horse people more or that he found the topic boring. The bitter fact is he knew that, for all his independence, he was more directly answerable to them than the rest of his friends. He worked for them. Although he and his men also painted and decorated ordinary people's houses, the real profit came from the jobs they did for the horse people; so he knew his job, his income, and therefore—as far as he was concerned—his destiny hung on making sure they were pleased with him and his work. The truth is he probably resented them even more, but he never let those sentiments come out. He may not even have been fully aware of them himself. He just avoided the subject.

In any case, in 1940 when I was eleven years old, the business failed. Collapsed. Went under. I am sure my father believed until the day he died that if he had just worked a bit harder, stayed an extra hour here or there, mixed the paint a trifle thinner, hounded a customer who hadn't paid his bill a little more persistently, it could have been saved. Like everyone else who "fails" in work because of the mysterious machinations of macroeconomic forces, he blamed himself. No one ever taught him how to look at the bigger picture. How could he have known—whose only reading was the Philadelphia *Inquirer, The Saturday Evening Post,* a trade journal for painters, and Ellery Queen detective novels—that his little business was collapsing because bigger businesses and chain stores were using "economies of scale," something he'd never heard of, to force him and thousands of small, self-employed entrepreneurs and independent artisans who owned their own tools—trucks, power saws, plastering trowels, jacks—to throw in the towel? All he knew was the paint cost more, factories were offering men better money than he could afford to pay them and customers were getting scarcer. One day he decided he couldn't take it any longer, sold the pickup truck and the ladders, and told us he was going to look for a job at the local steel tubing factory, on "one of the shifts."

That was hard for me to absorb. It was also my other lesson in class consciousness. Most of my friends' fathers and some of their mothers worked at the tubing factory which was the main source of employment in town. But *my* father did not work there, and that had always made me feel I was a little above them. Again, this subtle class outlook, what Marxists might see as that of a "Petit-bourgeois" toward proletarians, was never explicitly implanted. Somehow or other it was made known that even though we did not make any more money than they did—some years it was less—we were in some elusive way better off. We felt closer to the shift workers than to the horse people but we were still different. My father knew the factory workers well, but he preferred to play poker with a circle of friends, who, like him, were their own bosses—the owner of the local grocery store, the undertaker, the electrician, the plastering contractor. The word "proletarization" never entered my father's ears, and he would not have understood if it had. But he feared it. He knew it hung over him, and he was right. Eventually it got him.

As it turned out he did not take the shift job at the local factory. I am not sure but I believe the change in status endured right there in our hometown would have been just too humiliating. Instead he held out a few weeks longer, then took a job in a chemical plant in West Chester, seven miles away. Working there he could keep the actual conditions and duties of the new job a little quieter. He still left town for work in the morning and returned in the evening as he always had when he was painting. He could fudge a bit when people asked him just what he was doing, since no one else from Malvern worked at the same place. The job was not in town. The fact that now he had a timecard and was required to punch in by eight, that he could not slip off to the horse races in the afternoon, that he no longer had gleaming barns and fences to show off could be covered up a bit. The relative anonymity of the position masked the enormity of the demotion.

My father was already an anacronism when he mixed his first pail of paint, a self-employed man whose only advertisement was what people said about his work, who learned his trade from his father, and whose identity was not dictated by a giant company. The miracle is that he survived as long as he did, and the miracle was made a little easier to perform since painting and carpentry remained then—and still remain—among the last holdouts against the currents of centralization and concentration.

Yet his business failed, one of the many thousands recorded in the statistics of the Department of Commerce for that year and every year. His extension ladders he quietly sold to his friend Harry who could use them in his roofing business—which went under a few years later. I never knew where he sold the truck or who painted over his name on the side. He went to work "on a shift," sticking his card in the little time clock twice a day, dumped together with the other older refugees from the economic wars and with the recent high school graduates who would never know anything but life inside a magnanimous corporation.

He had only himself to blame—or so he must have thought. He had not been a paragon of the Protestant work ethic, and his casual approach to some aspects of his occupation haunted him afterward. He loved to run his fingers over a smoothly painted wall or a well papered ceiling. He took pride in driving by a country mansion and seeing the paint job—one he had done—still holding up well five winters later. But when a job was finished he did not leap assiduously into the next one. In the summer he took me flounder and croaker fishing off Cape May, renting a small rowboat and chopping the squid bait on the seat into hook size pieces. In the fall, faking an excuse note to my teacher, he carted me off to Havre de Grace in his 1936 Chevrolet and taught me about handicaps, longshots, and daily doubles. On the way home I was allowed to eat peanuts and drink Cokes at the bar while he sipped beer with his racetrack cronies. He played poker a couple nights a week. He never went to church—until after the business failed—and his only religious advice to me was, "Never become a fanatic." But after he sold his truck and ladders my father got old very quickly. His hair turned gray. He became more sedate and pensive. He did not clown around as much, hardly ever went to the horse races, and eventually started attending church.

I wonder why he did. Was there anything at all in those hymns about diadems and ebenezers, about an immortal invisible God, that touched him? Was it the "precious Saviour, still our refuge"? It is hard to tell. He never talked about it, never discussed the sermon (hardly anyone ever did) and if he sang the hymns at all he did so in a voice so soft I never heard it. I still don't know what coming back to church after the business failed meant to him in his inner spirit. Sometimes when I glanced at him in the pew beside me I thought I could see a mixture of sadness and searching, a look in his eyes that told me he was there because his other god had failed. The work on which he had pinned his hopes, his self-esteem, his place in the universe, had collapsed. Why had it happened? What was left? Who *was* he, anyway? A *shift* worker! What monstrous crime could he possibly have committed to merit this outrageous punishment? He may have been fumbling for answers. Yes, I think he went to church for consolation (not a bad reason) and because the failure of the business pushed him to the edge, raised questions no previous misfortune ever had.

Did he get any answers? I don't know. Maybe the garbled gospel he heard and the pietistic hymns we sang at least gave him the sense of a wider world of meaning in which, mysteriously, he still had a place even with the ladders gone. Maybe under the layers of moralizing that flowed from the pulpit he heard an occasional hint of good news, that God was not punishing him by taking away the buckets and the pickup; so he did not need to blame himself.

During the years since he died I have often reflected on the meaning my father's going back to church had not just for him, but for me. I think even then I had at least an inkling of what he was going through. I knew he was in pain. But I also felt angry that he was not getting whatever he was looking for, that somehow the church was failing him. When I was in divinity school I sometimes had fantasies of going back and being the minister of that same church. I wanted to reach my father. With my sturdy convictions about the relevance of the gospel to work and politics, equipped by my seminary training with a coherent and persuasive theology, surely *my* sermons would have reached him. *My* eloquence would have been able to get by his resigned and close-to-desperate look and to say a liberating, healing word. My father, I thought bitterly, having taken the embarrassing and humbling step of going back into a church he had left decades before, deserved something better than what he got. Also, my own pride was involved. Since I was going into the ministry and this was the only church he knew, I was afraid, given everything our little church lacked, he would think I was going to spend my life on something trivial and irrelevant. That is not what I wanted him to think. I wanted him to be proud of me.

Of course, I never became the minister of the Malvern Baptist Church. After my "liberal" Yale Divinity School education, I would probably never have been called there anyway. The congregation preferred a more homespun, conservative theology. But I have learned two things from the fantasy of serving the church my father attended and from the feelings that went with it. The first is that I was right: the local congregation *is* the critical locus of Christian life. Unless the gospel is preached and heard at the grass-roots, where ordinary people—some of whom have just lost a spouse, a job, or something—gather in the pews, then all the best theological production in the world is wasted. The TV evangelists and the religious book trade will never take the place of the congregation. Second, however, I was wrong: despite my anger about what he was not hearing at church, my father *was* getting something. This change of mind reflects my more recently acquired belief that no minister, no matter how ill-prepared, pedantic, boring or rambling, can completely obscure the gospel. Like the (ex opere *operato*) idea of the mass, valid despite the priest's qualities, when the biblical message is read and interpreted, miraculously something does get through.

Don't ask me why I believe this. Maybe it is a residual Baptist-evangelical belief in the power of the Word. Maybe it is because I have personally heard the gospel so often despite its horrible presentation. Maybe it is because I cannot accept the injustice that would result if only those people who are privileged to hear sparkling and sophisticated preaching ever really get the message.

My father died when I was twenty-five. During his last days he asked me once, when I was visiting him in the hospital, to pray. I was surprised, almost shocked. He had never done such a thing before. Who was now the father here by this bed, who the son? Who was ministering to whom? I awkwardly put my hand in his and somehow sputtered a prayer of sorts aloud. It was not easy. The words that came out seemed trite, unable by far to bear the full weight of all that was being said, not just to God but between us. A few days later he was dead. He never did know what hit him. But by screwing up his courage and asking me to pray he had been inviting me into his dying as in more carefree days at the seashore and at the racetrack he had invited me into his life. In a single gesture he had sought some consolation for himself but he had done far more: he confirmed my faith and created a link between us that permitted me to say good-bye to him with some small sense of completion. What else, finally, can a son expect from a father?

# 6
# Baptist Roots and Black Churches

In one of William Styron's early novels, *Set This House on Fire,* he depicts a perfectly dreadful, smug, self-indulgent, bigoted, and generally unattractive couple who live in the southern city where the plot takes place. They are the only Baptists in the book, at least the only white Baptists. Apparently Styron felt that the string of negative adjectives I have listed above somehow or another go naturally with being Baptist. If pressed, he and others might add tacky, conventional, massively repressed, tasteless, philistine, easily subject to emotional manipulation and probably ineptly dressed.

I am a Baptist. How many of the foregoing adjectives apply to me I will allow others to decide. What I do know is that although I did not really choose to be a Baptist, (it was the church next door), I have chosen to *remain* a Baptist. I would only stop being a Baptist if I stopped being a Christian altogether, and even then I might still be Baptist (as, it seems to me, many others are). I became a Baptist through accident of ancestry and the geographical proximity of a church. But why do I stay?

On previous pages of this journey log I have said that faith is always tied up with such things as class and color. My staying a Baptist has a lot to do with that. When I went to college, I was not overtly class conscious but I did find that the thoughtful, critical Christians I met were not Baptists. Some of them were Episcopalians. I once thought briefly about changing. I never did however, largely because for me to become an Episcopalian, after being raised to despise the horse people of Chester County, would have been sheer class treason. I would have been joining "them." Later, when I was at Yale Divinity School, I noticed that some of the students who came in as Baptists left as something else, usually a denomination higher on the socioeconomic scale. They claimed they did it for theological or liturgical reasons, of course; but I always suspected that a smidgin of social climbing and status-seeking also entered in. For me staying a Baptist meant staying with my own people, not "going over" to the Congregationalist; or the Unitarians or the Episcopalians. Although I often hated the theology I heard preached from Baptist pulpits (and still do) somehow my petit-bourgeois psyche feels at home in most Baptist congregations. I am "one of them" and the oneness goes deeper than mere theology.

What is Baptist theology anyway? No denomination on earth includes a wider spread. When I was a senior at Penn the head of the Religious Studies Department was Edwin Aubrey, a religious naturalist from the far left of the liberal-modernist spectrum. And he was a Baptist. The Baptist campus pastor who had once been a teaching assistant to Walter Rauschenbusch the (Baptist) founder of the Social Gospel movement was a liberal social activist with a streak of pietism. What other denomination with the possible exception of the Roman Catholic (and I doubt even that) can allow an Edwin Aubrey and a Jerry Falwell to wear the same label? And can throw in Jesse Jackson, Billy Graham, Martin Luther King, Jr., Harry Emerson Fosdick, and Aretha Franklin?

This list of names includes a couple that hint at another reason why I stay Baptist: the black Baptist churches. I am desperately sorry now that I never attended a service in the tiny black Baptist church across the tracks in my hometown. I did go occasionally to the A.M.E. Church, but then it was on *this* side of the tracks and everyone knew it was more respectable. It was not until I became Protestant chaplain at Temple University in 1953 that I "discovered" the black church and that discovery became one of the milestones in my faith journey. Here is how it happened.

Bored and sick of studying at divinity school after two years, I decided to take a year out. I found a job as Protestant chaplain at Temple University, a predominantly white school located in the heart of the North Philadelphia black ghetto. When I arrived at the university I discovered that according to registration statistics about half the students were Jewish and about a third were Catholic. That left slightly over 15 percent as my Protestant "flock" and I quickly found out that most of them were black . . . and Baptist. Since my work went on mainly during the week (it was a commuter school) and I had no regular Sunday morning responsibility, I began accompanying my students to their various churches, some of them small with names like Star of Hope Baptist or Pillar of Fire Baptist; others huge with names like Zion and Shiloh and Bethel.

There was never a dull Sunday. Each week I heard choirs, some with more people singing in them than were in the whole congregation of my home church, shake the walls with gospels and spirituals and anthems. I listened to preaching that turned the Bible into a contemporary drama and unashamedly mixed piety and politics. I stayed for a lot of dinners, was always welcomed and invited back, was sometimes asked to sit up with the preacher and bring a greeting. I do not ever remember being bored even once.

But there was something else that spoke to me in those black Baptist churches in the north Philadelphia of the 1950s. It was the fusion of the familiar and the strange. They sang the same hymns I had been raised on. Small wonder, since in the tinier churches the hymnbooks were often hand-me-downs from a white Baptist church that had bought new ones. But they sang them differently. It was not that the folks in my home church did not sing loud or even—some of them—sincerely; it was that in the black churches, the words to "What a Friend We Have in Jesus," "The Old Rugged Cross," and "Just as I Am" seemed to connect with something so urgent and so heartfelt that they leaped clearly beyond the sentimental lyrics themselves. I had met God and been "saved" in my own little church. But it was in the black churches that I came to know the power and profundity of my own tradition. Still, was it really "my" tradition? Eventually I learned—painfully—that in some respects it is not. I found out that although I can feel closer to God in a black Baptist church than in any other church, I really do not belong there, except as a visitor or guest. This was a hard lesson.

During the years we lived in Roxbury our family belonged to the Blue Hill Christian Church, a mixed congregation, whose black Baptist pastor was Virgil Wood, a consistently splendid preacher. When we moved out of Roxbury I occasionally attended black churches and still do. But I have come to believe that regardless of how hard I try to be a part, my being white prevents me from sharing fully in the worship of black people. Not because I ever have felt excluded or unwelcome. I never have. I cannot be a part because I cannot bring to the singing and praying the *collective* suffering and courage black people bring; and that is what makes black worship what it is.

I am not interested in romanticizing black worship, or in writing paeans to "soul." Affected as it is by its heritage of pietism, black worship can become maudlin and the preaching can become bombastic and overly bent on arousing effect. Still, what is vital about black worship is that the people in the pews bring their entire range of hopes and resentments into the sanctuary, not just some "religious" segment. And they come as a people, not merely as individuals. That is the secret of joy and even ecstasy white people find so fascinating and puzzling in black churches. It is not cheap joy, the equivalent of what

Bonhoeffer always condemned as "cheap grace." It is expensive joy, and the price of admission is high.

My experience in black churches, most of the them Baptist, has made an incalculable contribution to my faith journey. It has kept me a Baptist. But it has also taught me a lesson: that a luminous encounter with God in worship cannot be conjured up even by the finest liturgy, the most eloquent preaching or the music of the angels. Black worship makes me wonder what it would take to get the average, middle-class white congregation to become a people and not just a collection of individuals, and to bring all the raw edges of corporate life into the prayer and singing and listening. Not often, but once in awhile this happens in our own local white Baptist congregation. But mostly we revert to being individuals with little sense of shared destiny. Our competitive-accumulative society has bred its individualism into us very successfully. And often we revert to thinking of church as having to do with some fifth dimension of ourselves called the "spiritual." What we as whites have to learn from the black churches is not how we can emulate what it is that gives them their liveliness and power. Rather we need to learn how to take the risk of carrying a wider and deeper range of *our* human reality into the encounter with God. We need to bring our corporate guilt and rage and wild hope with us, setting aside some of our discretion and evasiveness. Black people can laugh and shout in church only because they can also moan and cry. And they can do it all because a history of being hurt and resisting has made them into a people.

There is a painful irony about the way I feel both at home and somehow not at home in black Baptist churches. In a Catholic Church I sense myself mostly as a welcome guest (at least usually welcome) in someone else's house. I can appreciate the strangeness. In the black Baptist church I sing the same hymns we sang in Malvern Baptist Church and I listen to the same lessons. But there is something strange. It is not the same. Something evil, maybe even demonic, is separating me from people with whom God meant me to be united. That diabolic presence does its damage even in the house of God, and I feel it more keenly than a visiting Catholic would precisely *because* the outer forms are so familiar. I cannot attribute the estrangement to unfamiliarity with the responsive readings, the decor, the altar call. I am familiar with them all. So I am forced to recognize that what makes me feel alien is the powerful persistence of racism, the deeply internalized poisoning of perception that distorts the vision of all of us, black and white (in different ways) and will continue to haunt us until it is uprooted and left behind.

Black churches do not exist to provide a theological challenge to white churches, or to supply some kind of inspiration to white Christians. They exist to bring the hope of the gospel into the lives of people whom history, including white Christian history, has tried to rob of hope. They exist as places where black people can band together to insure their survival and comfort one another with song and story. Still, just by being themselves, the black churches do challenge and inspire whites, even if this is not their intention. They do so, I think, by demonstrating what faith is like when it becomes a matter of survival, a question of life and death.

This total-claim quality of Christianity, something I think the black churches at their best represent, is another thing that keeps me a Baptist. Not that Baptists as they now exist in America stand any closer to this holistic practice than other denominations do. Indeed in many ways Baptists, having become the "culture religion" of large parts of the country, have lost it completely. Still, at the core of Baptist theology and life, and the element that gives Baptists their name, is the rite of total immersion. I believe that this seemingly outdated and even outlandish practice still conveys something immensely important. When Baptists betray what that total immersion symbol signifies, we betray what is indispensable to our tradition.

A couple of years ago I officiated at the baptism by immersion of a young woman who had been coming to our church for a few years and finally decided, as she put it, to "take the plunge." She asked me to preach that Sunday on baptism, so I took the slightly flippant double-entendre the young woman had used as the title of the sermon: "Taking the Plunge." What I said that day sums up what I believe about the meaning of baptism (and therefore of staying a Baptist, despite everything). I recall it here, from rumpled notes:

> In recent years our whole culture has begun to appreciate more and more the utter centrality of the body. We have bioenergetics, free dance, scream therapy, yoga, Tai Chi, psychodrama. Why then should baptism by immersion seem odd? In the language of the streets we talk about "really getting into it," "taking the plunge," "jumping in with both feet," "in over my head." We believe that faith is not just a matter of ideas, not a "head trip." We believe it involves the whole person, or so we say. If then faith has to do with all of our life—body, mind, and spirit—with hair and belly, eyes and ankles, then we can best signify the inclusive quality of our faith by a total gesture. We don't keep a finger or a toe out. We do not use a snorkle. We allow ourselves, all of ourselves, to be plunged below the foreboding and life-giving waters. We feel it from our soles to our scalps. It tells us in a way we will never forget what faith is about.

If this chapter has sounded a little narrow to the non-Baptist reader, or has confirmed all the worst things William Styron believes about Baptists, so be it. I seek no converts. I would never try to persuade someone to join a Baptist church rather than some other one. I do believe, however, that an integral part of our faith journey involves coming to terms with our own roots, however we dislike them, and deciding what to do with "where we have come from" before we discard it too easily. No doubt my journey has made me a different kind of Baptist than I was the day I was baptized. I am sure there are people in the world who are embarrassed to admit that I am a Baptist, just as it pains me to admit any links with them. But out of accident, inertia, conviction, and maybe a trace of perversity, that is what I still am and probably always will be. Amen, brother. Tell it like it is.

# 7
# The Berlin Wall
## 1962-63

In August 1962 a Lufthansa plane carrying my wife Nancy, me, and our two small children landed at Templehof Airport in West Berlin. We were met by my old seminary friend Bob Starbuck who had been working for a number of years as an Ecumenical Fraternal Worker in Berlin and whose place I was coming to take for a year. I had just finished my Ph.D. in history and philosophy of religion at Harvard. I spent the two previous years writing a long turgid dissertation ("Religion and Technology from the Renaissance to the Present") and was eager to get out of libraries and away from my writing desk. The activist side of my nature had languished over the hard years of doctoral study, and the invitation to go to Berlin seemed like a godsend.

My job in Berlin was to live in the western half of the divided city and work on "Ostcontakt," keeping lines of communication open with the eastern half. That meant, concretely, becoming a staff member of the Gossner Mission, a church-sponsored adult education center in East Berlin. I would teach, do research, meet with informal study groups and—most intriguing for me—become a part of the earliest stages of the "Christian-Marxist dialogue," a difficult but critically important conversation which was then just in its infancy.

How can I write about this influential year in my faith journey? I kept a daily journal, and someday I hope to publish it. But for now I have chosen two more fragmented ways of conveying the flavor of that year lived in the shadow of Die Mauer. On three occasions I was briefly detained and interrogated by East German border police and agents of the State Security Service. I have no idea what the reports of those interrogations said, but using a large dose of writer's license, I have tried here to imagine them. I must have been a puzzling case, a frequent border-crosser who was neither smuggling nor subverting. Also, during my stay in Berlin I met and became friends with a young Marxist intellectual, a Party member and teacher at the university of East Berlin whom I here call "Erich Wasserman." The memoranda are entirely fictional, and I have lost touch with "Erich." Still I hope that what follows will explain in some way why Berlin was such an important way station on my journey.

\* \* \* \* \*

Memorandum

TO: Oberleutnant Otto Foerster, Intelligence Division, Berlin Volks-Polizei
FROM: Leutnant Siegfried Kresge, Chief, Interrogation Section, Border Police
October 22, 1962

The subject about whom you requested information, Harvey Cox, was detained at the Fredrichstrasse border crossing point ["Checkpoint Charlie"] yesterday morning, Oct. 21, 1962, as he sought to enter East Berlin carrying a valid American passport. Subject was entering legally, observing all requisite conditions. He was carrying no contraband as a

thorough search of his person indicated. He did have a paper
sack filled with oranges and apples and several chocolate candy
bars which he said were gifts for the family of a pastor he said
he was going to visit, in the Weissensee section of East Berlin.
He was also carrying two volumes of *Kircheliche Dogmatik* by
Karl Barth and a Bible dictionary. Although the importation of
unregistered literature into the German Democratic Republic
is officially illegal, the books seemed sufficiently obscure not to
constitute any danger to the populace. He said he was taking
them as a gift to the same pastor.

Since the subject has crossed the border at this point and also
at the Bahnhof Fredrichstrasse checkpoint several times in
recent weeks, always legally, and has always returned within
the twenty-four-hour period alloted, there seemed to be no
reason to hold him further. When interrogated, he claimed he
was an "Ecumenical Fraternal Worker" assigned to the
Protestant Church of Berlin-Brandenburg with special responsibility for maintaining communication with the Gossner
Mission (an adult education center related to the Protestant
church) and to the Evangelical Academy. Subject appears to
receive no pay from either organization but is supported by his
own church through an arrangement with the Gossner Mission
in West Berlin. His documents indicate that he resides in West
Berlin at 131 Bundesallee with his wife Nancy, also an
American citizen, and his two small children, Rachel (3) and
Martin (1).

Subject appears to have no connection with the CIA or with
any other organ of American Intelligence. Our operatives
have observed him and his wife twice at the Berthold Brecht
Theatre on Schiffsbauerdamm, once for a production of
*Mother Courage* and once for an open rehearsal of *The Good
Woman of Setzuan*. He has also been observed at churches and
conferences, drinking beer and eating wurst at small restaurants with groups of our citizens, and once or twice at the home
of a somewhat obscure artist whose name we are now checking
on but who seems to specialize in woodcuts of scenes from the
Bible. Subject also once visited the archaeology section of the

State Museum but appeared bored (as reported by Operative #2765 who works as a guard there) and left after a few minutes.

During questioning the subject appeared a little nervous but no more so than one would expect under the circumstances. He answered all questions forthrightly, or so it appeared to us. His German, though somewhat weak, is passable. He seems to understand everything that is asked but has difficulty replying if the answer requires the use of past tenses or subjunctive moods.

\* \* \* \* \*

Memorandum

TO: Oberleutnant Otto Foerster, Intelligence Division, Berlin Volkspolizei
FROM: Leutnant Siegfried Kresge, Chief, Interrogation Section, Border Police December 18, 1962

As you requested, subject Harvey Cox was intercepted again at the Bahnof Fredrichstrasse checkpoint, as he entered East Berlin legally with a valid American passport. The subject, again, was carrying no contraband. He did have with him four small Christmas fruitcakes, some homemade cookies, a knitted scarf (gift wrapped), and still more copies of Karl Barth's *Kircheliche Dogmatik.* He also had a copy of Dietrich Bonhoeffer's *Widerstand und Ergebung* and a two-week-old copy of *Die Zeit* [a newspaper published in Hamburg]. Since the newspaper appeared to be used principally to wrap the fruitcakes however, it is unlikely that it was being smuggled into the German Democratic Republic contrary to public law #7R-9473. Subject was also carrying a small pocket-sized German-English dictionary and a personal address book. A check of the addresses listed revealed no suspect names or connections.

When questioned, subject claimed he was going to attend "a

Bible study and Christmas party" in a church meeting center in the Kreuzekirche. The report of Operative #5373, assigned to follow him after he was released, indicates that is in fact what he did. The gathering seemed to be of university students, probably connected with the Student Christian Movement. They sang several Christmas carols, had a discussion on "Living as a Christian in a Socialist Country" led by the student-pastor, ate a meal of boiled potatoes, beans, coffee, and pudding and then sat and talked in small groups. Subject entered into the discussion but did not seem to be leading it.

Also during the questioning, subject said, in response to a direct question, that he did not think it was any harder to be a Christian in East Germany than in the U.S., since it is not easy anywhere and the difficulties, though different in different countries, evened out in the long run, that the "materialism" of the West was in its own way more subtle and misleading than the "materialism" of the East. He also said, in response to a question, that he agreed with his East German Christian friends who had decided not to leave for the West since "that would leave no one to interpret the gospel to the Marxists."

Since his previous interrogation, subject has traveled once to Paris (as indicated by stamp on his passport). When asked about the trip, he replied that he had gone there to attend a meeting sponsored by the World Council of Churches. Intelligence confirms that such a meeting was actually held in Paris at that time. Subject also admitted that he had not spent his entire time at the World Council of Churches meeting but had also visited two museums, three art galleries, and a Bohemian night club on the Montmartre which features cabaret singers and apache dancers.

Also since his last interrogation subject has paid two visits to the home of Comrade Erich Wassermann, a member of our Communist party and a part-time lecturer at the university here in East Berlin. We had already had reports from another operative about these meetings. They seem to have little interest for us since the two apparently spend their time drinking Bulgarian wine, eating cheese and wurst sandwiches, and arguing about the existence of God. They both seem to enjoy the conversations and apparently try to trip each other up on quotations from Marx, Kant, Bloch, and Barth. Since Comrade Wassermann teaches courses on the "Marxist Critique of Religion" it is not surprising that these two men should carry on such useless discussions. It might be worth checking with Comrade Wasserman's chief, however, to determine whether his afternoons might be better spent than in disporting himself in such a manner while so many of our hardworking citizens have so little time for such things. It also appears to us that if Comrade Wassermann feels that the subject, Mr. Cox, might eventually turn out to be a valuable source of intelligence on political matters or that he might be involved in some form of intelligence gathering we believe the comrade is, so to speak, barking up the wrong tree, in both respects.

Subject's German has definitely improved. Maybe he is getting used to being interrogated. He is now able to use the past tenses with little difficulty although he still has considerable trouble with subjunctives. When asked why his German was better than the last time he was questioned, he (jokingly) replied that it all came from reading our Communist Party newspaper *Neues Deutchland* which, he said, was written in such unreadable style that he had to study it with dictionary and grammar book in hand. Our interrogation officer assured him that we did not think that was a very funny remark. He also claimed that he worked on his German by using the West Berlin telephone services which provide recorded messages about weather, food prices, movie programs, sports results, and news summaries. He maintains that he simply dials these recorded messages over and over and repeats them back until he has them memorized, then rushes down to the cafe on the ground floor of his apartment house to converse with the patrons about weather, sports, food prices, and movies. The explanation sounded implausible, but we let it pass.

Our office confesses that it is still unclear about what really motivates the subject to continue coming to East Berlin so frequently, three or four times a week, to attend Bible studies, church services, religious conferences, and theological study groups. He does not seem to be smuggling anything nor to be intent on subverting our state. It seems odd that church people find it this important merely to keep communication and personal contact between East and West, but we have no other explanation for his activities.

During this interrogation the subject seemed calmer than during the first one, even though he had had to wait for two hours at the checkpoint detention center until a competent interrogator could be found to question him. He was observed to spend the time reading one of the theological books he was carrying and did not seem to be bored or nervous during the wait. He did go to the lavatory once and we thought he might use the occasion to try to flush some documents or letters down the toilet (he had not yet been thoroughly searched), but according to Operative #267 who monitors these things, no such attempt was made.

When the subject was released he seemed relieved. He wished the interrogation officer a "Merry Christmas" and offered all the guards small pieces of the fruitcake he was carrying. This offer was, of course, respectfully refused according to provision #298 of the Official Handbook for interrogation procedures which explicitly excludes accepting any form of gift from any person being interrogated.

* * * * *

Memorandum

TO: Oberleutnant Otto Foerster, Intelligence Division, Berlin Volkspolizei
FROM: Leutnant Siegfried Kresge, Chief, Interrogation Section, Border Police April 23, 1963


I can understand your skepticism about why Harvey Cox, still resident at 131 Bundesallee in West Berlin, continues to cross into East Berlin three or four times a week quite openly at the legal checkpoints. Your theory that he must be engaged in some questionable activity or that he is in some way subverting our state might seem persuasive at first but there are a number of sound reasons to doubt it. If he is doing something pernicious, why does he enter and leave so openly, always observing the legal requirements for such movement? Why have our interrogations and searches turned up no evidence of subversive intent? Why have our operatives and informants who have checked on the meetings he attends and the lectures he gives to the classes he is teaching at the Gossner Mission not been able to produce any incriminating evidence?

I realize it seems surprising that anyone should so persistently continue to visit our side of this divided city especially during the extremely cold weather we have just had this past winter. But all theories of his being paid by some questionable source or his being part of a conspiracy to confuse and mislead people, especially church people, here in our state, seem so far unproven. Our informants tell us that in his classes here he does not exhort people to leave East Germany or laud the West in seductive terms. He seems to try to help them pull together for the good of everyone and to be examples of what he calls "Christian presence" to their fellow workers, neighbors, and friends. Although our questioning reveals that he is definitely a Christian believer and not an atheist, he insists that a "dialogue" between Christians and atheists is possible and that Christians should not enter into it self-righteously but humbly. He seems to know something about Marx (much of which he has apparently learned since he has been here) and is willing to criticize certain features of Marxism but still seems to take it seriously as something he should know about.

At his most recent interrogation (yesterday, at Checkpoint Charlie) he gave substantially the same information he had given in the two previous interrogations. At one point he even offered some answers to questions that the officer had not yet asked since he seemed to know what was coming next. This understandably confused the interrogation officer who had only been on this type of duty for two months. The officer was a little nervous. (I observed this since I stayed in the room during the questioning to make sure your concerns were covered.) At one point the subject seemed to be trying to put the interrogation officer at ease and said something like, "Don't worry, you'll eventually get the hang of how this is done." This was a little embarrassing to the officer, but I assume in a few months he will be able to deal with such situations more easily.

Again the subject was carrying a volume of Karl Barth's *Kircheliche Dogmatik* in German. He claimed that it was not a gift but for reading on buses. Although this seemed improbable to us, we again did not consider the book to be dangerous to the general populace. In fact neither the interrogating officer nor I could understand a single paragraph of it.

* * * * *

Memorandum

TO: Oberleutnant Otto Foerster,
Intelligence Division,
Berlin Volkspolizei
FROM: Leutnant Siegfried Kresge,
Chief Interrogation Section, Border Police
July 10, 1963

This is to inform you that yesterday Harvey Cox, the subject of three previous reports, stopped at the office of the detention section here while I was gone and left a message that he and his family were leaving this week for America. His message said that he wished us all well, that he had gotten to enjoy what he called "our little conversations," and that he hoped we would meet again some day.

\* \* \* \* \*

Herr Erich Wassermann
117 Manfriedstrasse
Berlin 45
German Democratic Republic (East Germay)

Aug 13, 1981

Dear Erich,

It has been five years now since my last visit to Berlin and our seeing each other. It is now nearly nineteen years since my year in Berlin in 1962-63 as an Ecumenische Mitarbeiter which was generally translated as "Ecumenical Fraternal Worker." But you will of course have noticed instantly the date on which I write this letter, and you will know just as instantly what it means.

*Today is the twentieth anniversary of the building of The Wall.*

I was not, of course, in Berlin that day. I arrived one year later, just in time to hear the angry horn-blowing and protest that marked the first anniversary. I also quickly learned that real, toughened, sophisticated Berliners do not make much of The Wall. Tourists flocked to see it then and still do, I'm sure. Visiting American politicians had the mandatory photo taken of themselves staring grimly into the "East Zone" from the rickety wooden platform on the Potsdam Plaza. But we who lived in those days in its shadow did not talk about it very much. And those of us who crossed through the border often learned to appear blasé about it to visitors. We cultivated the same coolness medical students affect toward their cadavers. Was it for the same reason? Did we assume that bored look when visitors queried us about The Wall because if we did not we might cry, or release a volcano of feelings we were barely holding at bay?

In any case, I arrived in Berlin in the summer of 1962 as you will surely remember, to become part of a small team of Christians from the U.S. and Western Europe. Our task was to maintain contact between church organizations, families, and individuals who had become separated by The Wall. It is hard to explain to people nowadays just how difficult that was, or even why it was necessary. People forget, or never knew, that the U.S. did not recognize East Germany then as a sovereign state. Your country was still officially referred to as the "Soviet Occupied Zone" or more frequently in West Berlin simply as "Die Zone." This meant that every time I crossed through Checkpoint Charlie from West Berlin to East Berlin (which I was permitted to do by the Four-Power Agreement, the legal basis on which our little group of Christian couriers worked), I was handed an official, printed warning by the American soldiers stationed there that I was entering territory in which my government "could not accept any responsibility" for my "safety or security." After a while I stopped taking the notice. I knew it by heart. But somewhere in my mind I remembered it whenever I was in your country. Truthfully, Erich, I never did feel fully safe or secure.

Also back in those early days after The Wall, there were no telephone lines between the two severed halves of the city. Telegrams and letters were monitored. And, above all, there was no travel—by Berliners—between the two sides of the city. As you know, that brought with it much sadness. Weddings, funerals, holidays, sicknesses, and personal crises took place with families unable to meet or even to speak with one another. The Lutheran Church, still organized on a city-wide basis, had to rely heavily on foreign "couriers" like myself and my friends to keep communication open. It was a tricky and demanding assignment. Sometimes I found myself trying to interpret to a study group of pastors in the East what a comparable study group in the West had meant by a letter or statement, or even what some individual's remark might have meant. It was touchy, and I made mistakes, especially early in the year when my German was not very good.

Remember how we met, early in the fall, after I had been in Berlin a couple of months? We were both guests at the home of a young instructor at the theological faculty of the Humboldt University in East Berlin. He knew that you, as an adjunct professor at the same university, teaching the Marxist critique of religion, liked to meet theologians. We soon discovered that we shared an interest in the philosophy of Ernst Bloch. You had to be a little careful in admitting that. Bloch had lived and taught in East Germany for awhile. But he was, although a brilliant Marxist thinker, too much of a free spirit for most of your bureaucratic comrades in the "Socialist Unity Party" (the official name of what is actually the Communist Party of your country). So old Ernst Bloch "defected" and went to West Germany where he taught in Tübingen until his death as an advanced octogenarian a few years ago. By the way, I forgot to tell you when we met in Berlin five years ago that I met Bloch just before his death at a conference in Vienna where he and Ivan Illich and I were giving papers on "The Future of Religion." Bloch and Illich seemed to hit it off well. (They are both utopians, after all.) I got into a rather loud altercation with Illich who was already pushing his radical criticism of the whole idea of economic development. (I later came to agree with some of what he was saying.) Bloch told me had read a couple of my books and liked them because he had a preference for "heretical theology" (he called it "Schwär-mertheolgie"). I told him I appreciated his compliment but that calling me a heretical theologian would probably not help much where I needed it most.

Well, back to Berlin. Bloch and I had just the same kind of rambling conversation you carry on, and I wish you could have been there with us. You were the one who once said to me, when I asked you if you accepted the Marxist idea about the "withering away of religion," that you did accept it, but that you believed religion would probably be around for about another thousand years! We opened another bottle over that one.

I also knew, although we never talked about it together, that you were a sort of consultant to the East German State Security Service on matters of religion and, more particularly, of religious personages who came into East Berlin. Therefore, during the three times I was detained and interrogated at The Wall, although I was a little upset (as who would not?) I felt some assurance that if the police ever checked me out with you, I would be okay. What I did not know, however, was just how secure, in the shifting and uncertain sands of inner party politics, *you* were. Intellectuals, even those who were party members, were not, as I recall, viewed without suspicion. And those who had frequent contacts with people from the West were viewed with more suspicion than others. I had a bad moment during my last interrogation when it occurred to me that there might have been an internal party coup, that you and your more "liberal" colleagues had been swept out, or even accused of complicity with the West, and that I was a patsy who would make a useful fall guy as one of your alleged "West contacts." When that thought occurred to me in the Interrogation Room I tried to get it out of my mind because I was also remembering the warning leaflet issued at Checkpoint Charlie telling all U.S. citizens that they were entering East Berlin at their own risk.

Well, needless to say, I was released that time, and the other times as well, but never without carrying with me a tiny bitter taste on the end of my tongue. Yes, I am still stubbornly "Western" and even "bourgeois" in some respects: I resent anyone's assuming the right to detain and interrogate me at any border, anywhere. The docile way hundreds of thousands of people a day submit themselves to this colossal humiliation always infuriates me. It seems like a pusillanimous surrender to the crazy idea that "sovereign states" can hack up the surface of God's globe into fenced-in precincts and then station bullies and incipient masochists to patrol these "borders," a job to which such people seem alarmingly well-suited.

Don't think I am singling out your country for some unique culpability. I was once strong-armed at the Boston Airport and rushed into a search-and-interrogation room just after I had arrived on an international flight from Mexico City. I was younger then, and I also still wore a beard (which I have shaved off since it started turning gray). I'm sure the guys who pushed me into that little curtained chamber (those rooms look the same everywhere; I've been in a number of them) suspected I was carrying drugs. They found nothing of course, but what infuriated me was that after they let me go I began to feel a kind of gratitude toward them. Gratitude! Why? For not killing or torturing or imprisoning me? It's a troubling question. Why should people who are misused and insulted feel some gratitude that their mistreatment was not even worse? Would reflecting on this unattractive quality in me teach me anything about the totalitarian mentality that lurks in all of us?

All that aside, Erich, perhaps reserved for our next talk, what I really wanted to write you about was a conviction that has come over me in the past few years; namely, that we have *both* been left behind by the sweep of history. Berlin, Erich, is *not* where the action is anymore. The critical confrontation in the world today is not the one between the old men who run the USSR and (personal company excepted) the German Democratic Republic on the one hand, and the U.S.A. on the other. Reagan and Brezhnev are both relics, dangerous and overarmed relics, but relics. They see the world through granny glasses ground in a bygone era. The hard new fact for both the USA and the USSR and their so-called "allies" (all of whom, both East and West, seem less willing every day to be servile satellites) is that the real confrontation is now going on somwhere else. I do not believe anyone in our Pentagon really believes Soviet tanks are about to roll toward Hamburg or Munich. The real rivalry between our two empires is taking place in the Third World, and speaking as someone who has lived a good deal in that world in the past decade, I know the people do not want to belong to either empire. As my Nicaraguan friend Ernesto Cardenal says, "We don't want a Russian revolution or a Chinese revolution or a Cuban revolution. We want a Nicaraguan revolution."

I am afraid, old friend, we have been upstaged. History is not being made these days, as we sometimes thought it was back then, at the intersection of Potsdamerallee and Alexanderplatz. How heady it was in those halcyon months to wake up every morning thinking the world's attention was focused on us. *Us.* Our Berlin, a big city but a tiny place on the globe.

It was lively all right. Your Russian-built MIGs buzzed American planes coming in for landings at Templehof. Tanks rumbled through the streets on what seemed like constant alert. John F. Kennedy flew in and said, in German with a Boston accent, "Ich bin ein Berliner!" Why we hardly had to *do* anything, Erich. Just *being* in Berlin in those days seemed like enough. If Berlin is calmer now, more relaxed, I am sure that is a good thing. Can I confess to you however that just once in awhile I furtively long for those days of venturesome wall crossings, semi-clandestine meetings that seemed almost like trysts, tension, endless argumentation about Marxism, Christian theology, politics, and the meaning of life. All going on in the city that everyone said was the world frontier between East and West.

Well, not only have we been upstaged, Erich, our discussion has been left behind too. After the Gdansk strike, the rise of Solidarity which, knowing you, I suspect you secretly admire and approve of although you will surely never be able to admit it . . . after all this can you still really believe that you live in a country of what you used to call "established socialism"? Do you feel a little pained that it is Catholics, not Communists, who are leading the revolution in Latin America?

You have a lot of homework to do, Erich. Religion it turns out, has not become the opiate of the masses everywhere, but has become in some places a kind of stimulant, a catalyzer of social change. My friends in Nicaragua tell me that the Cubans who go there to teach or work in clinics are often dumfounded when they discover that the Christians are the backbone of the revolution. Since the Cubans come from a country in which, as in yours, the revolutionary fervor is running at a low ebb, they cannot help wondering about some of the things they were taught about religion. Some have even joined the Catholic Church. (This by the way would come as a terrible shock to Alexander Haig who seems to believe that Cuba is unduly influencing Nicaragua when the truth is quite the other way around.)

So, as we say here, Erich, it's a new ballgame. The philosophical tenor of the discussions we had in the sixties about Christianity and Marxism does not interest my Latin American friends much. They think of Marxism as a useful tool, among others, to understand the nature of their bondage and deprivation. Their inspiration comes not from Marx or Lenin however, but from Jesus, the prophets and the words and example of the exemplary figures in their own history— people like Bishop Valdivieso of Nicaragua who was martyred three centuries ago for siding with the Indians, or Bartolomeo de las Casas who carried the battle for the rights of the Indians back to the king of Spain, or Camilo Torres or Oscar Romero. The revolution there is proceeding not by imposing a theory on the poor but by what my friends call "accompanying the poor" and learning from them. That's a far cry from the kind of tea table Marxist-Christian dialogue that went on between you and me in "Unser Berlin." Today's Wall runs between North and South, not between Unter den Linden and Tiergarten.

Still, I am not sorry, Erich. The talks I had with you prepared me in some measure for the experience I have had in Latin America. And, above all, I think that you and I, despite The Wall that separated our world views as well as our places of residence in Berlin, found that there was no wall between *us*. We became, despite everything, friends. And friends we remain. And though The Wall has now been standing for twenty years, we proved to each other—without ever saying it—that it could not ultimately keep *us* apart. I think it never will.

Sincerely,
Harvey

# 8
# The Roxbury Years

We moved to Roxbury in 1963 on a gray November day. The cardboard boxes of paperbacks, the folding chairs and the used mattresses squeezed easily into a rented U-Haul trailer which friends helped us load and unload. We ate our first supper, an egg omelette topped off with desert of sweet potato pie from the local Black Muslim bakery, off a card table. As night fell, Nancy and I looked at each other with a mixture of satisfaction and apprehensiveness. We had just bought this house and moved our family (Rachel 4, Martin 3, and Sarah on the way) into the predominantly black section of Boston. We were in the "ghetto."

A decade later it is hard to remember honestly all the factors that entered into what most of our friends and relatives looked on as a bizarre if not totally crazy decision. "Move *into* Roxbury?" people would say to us in amazement, "but everybody's moving *out!*" But we had our reasons. We had already become familiar with the area through the Blue Hill Christian Center, an inner-city ministry I helped organize a year earlier. We found ourselves commuting between Roxbury and our apartment in Newton once or twice a day and we wanted to live closer. We had gotten bored with the tedium and sameness of the suburbs. Our family was growing and we needed more room, and big houses in Roxbury were selling for half what they cost in Newton. Further, we wanted to make a statement about racial integration (that it does not go just one way), raise our children in a racially inclusive setting and (I think it is honest to say), do something a little reckless and venturesome, maybe to counteract the premature senility of the soul that can begin to set in at thirty-five or so as children, mortgages, and career-building begin to drain off the bubbling effervescence of the twenties.

We lived in Roxbury until June 1970, through the rise and fall of the Civil Rights Movement, the ghetto revolts, the deaths of John and Robert Kennedy, of Malcom X and Martin Luther King, Jr., the waxing and waning of the Great Society, the debacle of the war on poverty, the election of Richard Nixon and the escalation of the Vietnam War. During those years Nancy acted in various Boston theatres, taught science at an inner-city school, and worked as press secretary for a congressional campaign. I taught first at Andover Newton, then at Harvard, and worked at the Blue Hill Christian Center.

The Center was named after Blue Hill Avenue, the main thoroughfare of Roxbury which begins near Dudley Station and veers several miles south to Mattapan. In the 1960s it was lined with mom-and-pop stores, bars, storefront churches, delicatessens, and gas stations. We lived in the Grove Hall district of Blue Hill Avenue, near where Roxbury abuts on Dorchester, a previously Jewish area. It had street after tree-lined street of apartment houses, tenements, and one-, two- and three-family homes.

The Center itself, inspired by the East Harlem Protestant Parish and other inner-city urban ministries of the time, occupied the second floor of a row of stores on the corner of Blue Hill Avenue and Quincy Street. It included a continuing education section, a regular Sunday congregation, a fabulous "Freedom Choir," a street-level room for impoverished alcoholic men, a social action office, a dance and recreation room and lots of heart. It was a controversial, pulsating, highly visible center of the tumultuous events that seethed through Roxbury and the nation in the sixties. I am glad my family and I were there in the middle of it all.

The Blue Hill Christian Center was the site of the founding of the first chapter of Martin Luther King's Southern Christian Leadership Conference north of the Mason-Dixon Line. The Boston SCLC consisted of a few local black clergy in the leadership spots and a few white ministers as the members. The president was the Rev. Virgil Wood, a black Baptist minister from Virginia who had worked with SCLC in the South.

Four weeks after the founding of the Boston SCLC, King called us one fine October day and invited us to dispatch a delegation of our members, especially the white ministers, to a little town called Williamston in North Carolina where the local SCLC chapter was running into trouble in its efforts to desegregate the restaurants, get blacks into the white schools, or even hold public marches without harassment. The Williamston SCLC leadership had initiated the invitation. They obviously hoped that the visible presence of northern white ministers might give them both moral support and some protection against police clubs. Some of us in the newly formed Boston SCLC agreed to go to Williamston for a few days, join in the demonstrations and sit-ins, and help wherever we could. It was the sixties, and it seemed like the right thing to do. Even after all the later criticism of northern "do-gooders," I still think it was; after all we were *invited* by fellow Christians. We were guests.

When I arrived in Williamston in early November I stayed at the home of Sarah Small, the local SCLC president, and one of the most courageous people I have ever met. She kept a radio with gospel music playing most of the time and had floodlights placed around her house so no one could sneak close enough to fire a shot. She sang to herself a lot. She is the "Sarah" for whom our younger daughter, who was born after my return from Williamston, is named.

Sarah Small was working at that time with a brilliant, hyperactive and sometimes impulsive SCLC leader named Golden Frinks. Golden was not from Williamston but from a town eleven miles away and was therefore an "outside agitator." The local whites also referred to him as "the biggest liar in the whole county." They had a point. Golden could stretch the truth a mite here and there, as I quickly learned, but part of this was a strategy to keep the white power elite confused about just how many people were going to be involved in any demonstration, when and where things were happening, who had said what to whom, and so forth. Also, Golden was not above interpreting the situation to visiting white clergy with, occasionally, something less than utter candor. He was simply given to hyperbole. Still he had an engaging smile and an uncany sense of timing and tactical shrewdness. Somehow I trusted him even when I knew he was putting everyone on a bit, including me.

King himself never came to Williamston. He was busy leading demonstrations elsewhere and I had to wait for Selma and St. Augustine to work with him directly. Still we were in touch with him on the phone every day. Small sit-ins led to arrests, more and more interest, and an ever-tenser atmosphere in the town until finally Golden decided to organize a nonviolent march on the city hall itself. It was to be the Big One, the move that would turn the tide for Williamston blacks.

It was when the "big march" was announced that rumors of the folk from the hills appearing with their ax handles began to filter through to us as we met every night for prayer and singing and testimonies in the black church. It soon began to appear to many of us that it could be a replay of Gandhi's famous salt march in which the British simply knocked down row after row of nonviolent marchers with clubs. I felt my enthusiasm waning. I had no way of knowing that back in Roxbury Nancy and the other wives of the white ministers with me had called and put pressure on the governor of North

Carolina, Terry Sanford, who had then ordered the state
police to be on the scene and to see to it that nothing ugly
happened. They were. And nothing did. But we were all
arrested, sixty of us, including eleven white ministers.

The jail was unpleasant. They are for anyone, but I have a
touch of claustrophobia and hearing a door slam and lock from
the other side turns my blood to ice water every time. Also,
since we had been segregated from the black marchers who
had been arrested with us, we began a fast or hunger strike in
the jail to demand to be integrated. For three days the jail
authorities ignored, or pretended to ignore, the fact that we ate
none of our meals. The fast was harder for some of us than for
others. I did not like it at all. At every mealtime my stomach
would dutifully churn up the regular acids and enzymes which
then only surged and gurgled as they tried to digest each other.
I got unbearable headaches. Many years later, when the Irish
Republican Army prisoners fasted to death in 1981, I followed
the news every day with a kind of personal empathy my friends
could not understand. It is difficult to imagine a harder way to
die.

On the other hand, my cell mate, Warren McKenna, an
Episcopal priest from Boston, did not seem to be bothered by
hunger at all, at least outwardly. Every time the guards
brought a meal and placed it on the counter in the cell block,
yelling "Here's your lunch, preachers," all the rest of us would
move to the other side of the cellblock, as far away from the
sight and aroma of the food as we could get. Not Warren. He
would immediately saunter over to the counter and lift the lids
of the pans and say, "Hmm. Here's what we *would* have had for
breakfast this morning: coffee, oranges, hot grits." He did this
in good humor, to break the pall of monotony that often hangs
like a stifling miasma over jails. Usually, however, someone
would eventually say, "Okay, Warren, cut it out!" and he would
return from the counter, light a cigarette (not included in the
fast) and tell yet another joke or anecdote. After an hour or so
the guards would come and carry away the untouched food.

As one day turned into another and we refused meal after

meal, I felt increasingly testy and irritable. On the third day at suppertime, when Warren walked over to describe the food the guards had left, I lay on my bunk, put my fingers in my ears and sloshed the saliva around in my mouth so I would not hear the description. I was beginning to wonder if any of my fellow demonstrators and hunger strikers was beginning to feel as miserable about this as I was. How long would it be before I would break the solidarity, run over to the counter while the food sat there and wolf some down, or maybe find some way to sneak over, pretend only to look like Warren did, then hide a roll, an apple, in my pocket and gnaw on it later? I also wondered idly how Gandhi had ever fasted for forty days.

Finally on the afternoon of our fourth day, when all I could think about most of the day and dream about at night was food, the warden gave in and announced he was moving four of us white prisoners to the black section. I was one of the four. We cheered. The jail was the first institution in Williamston to be desegregated: a bizarre symbol.

When the four of us got to the black section of the jail, however, we quickly lost our euphoria at the breakdown of Jim Crow in the hoosegow. The black side was far more crowded, and there was no place for us to sleep. The food was poorer, was served more haphazardly, and there was less of it. Besides, by the time we got to where it had been placed, there was often none left. One black prisoner, who noticed I had had no lunch and also knew I had been fasting in the other cellblock, gallantly gave me half his dry cheese sandwich. Never will I forget the exquisite flavor of that dessicated morsel. It was the first food I had tasted in four days. I took twenty-five minutes to finish it, letting every crumb dissolve on my tongue.

There were other differences on the "black side." Although everyone in the white side of the jail had been incarcerated because of the march, a number of black prisoners were there on other charges. One older man kept shaking his head and staring at us whites. He seemed totally unable to understand why we were in the jail at all and especially in the black section. "Shit," he kept saying, then laughing and slapping his leg and looking at us, "shit! What you white boys doin' in here? Whatcho' in here for? Where you from?" One of my fellow white preacher-inmates, Paul Stagg, who had grown up in Mississippi, tried to explain. The man listened patiently but after the explanation he still shook his head in incredulity and laughed. The next day when I innocently asked him what he was in for, his answer was very straightforward. He had, he said, killed a man with a knife a few weeks before. Jails have a way of broadening one's range of social contacts.

When we eventually got out of jail I discovered that Andover Newton Theological School had proceeded with my installation as assistant professor of theology and culture, an event which I assumed would be postponed due to my not being able to be there, with me *in absentia*. My wife, Nancy, made the address at the ceremony and talked about the theologians from Paul to Bonhoeffer who had spent time behind bars. Although she may have played it up a bit more than it was worth, still she made a good point. Being in jail changes everyone who experiences it in one way or another.

Jail taught me something about power and weakness. In a jail you never quite forget, even for a moment, that if you are ever going to get out, it will be someone *else*, not you, who will open the door (unless you are constantly scheming escape, which—I'm told—longtimers do). I also learned some unattractive things about myself in jail. I was not a model prisoner, or even a good cellmate. I quickly became edgy with my fellow prisoners. I got tired of their jokes and sick of the sound of their voices. I felt lethargic and moody. I had no enthusiasm for the hunger strike, especially after the second day when the headache closed its clamps. Being in jail was no fun and I would not like to spend any time in jail again. I need to acquire self-knowledge in small, more easily digestible doses.

Still, jail was a critical stop on my faith journey. After a few hours I began to sense a peculiar kinship with the jailers, to detect an element of co-humanity in them. One assistant warden even told me, through the bars late one night, when he came by to check the cell and I was still awake, that he was "sick and tired of doing all the dirty work for them bastards up on the hill" (the wealthy section of town) and that he knew "a lot of the niggers in town are better people than they are by a damn sight." He lit a cigarette and we talked about our families. When he left I knew my stereotype of red-neck cops and cracker jailers needed reexamining.

Every year, on the anniversary of those days in the Williamstown jail, I sit alone somewhere and try to recall the whole thing with all its original nastiness, uncontaminated by the romantic layers I added later. Then, I try to think of the thousands of prisoners in the gulags of the USSR, the political security camps of Argentina and the death rows of the USA. My time in jail convinced me that when Jesus said the gospel must be good news for the prisoners or it is not really the gospel, it is these people he was talking about. People in jail are not interested in spiritual or internal liberation. They want *out*. How to make the gospel good news for them must be one of the most urgent tasks of any theologian or preacher. Once you hear that door slam, you always know it.

When I got back to Roxbury after Williamston, having been touted as something of a celebrity by the press ("Theology Professor Installed While in Cooler"), I learned something else. My black neighbors were not nearly as impressed as my white liberal friends were by my—very brief—imprisonment. For blacks, going to jail did not gain you any points and was something to be avoided, not courted as I had done. Also, they knew, but did not say right out, that going to jail for a few days was a lot easier for a white professor whose "record" would not be used against him the next time he looked for a job or an apartment in a public housing project. Although for the black friends who were most committed to the freedom movement, my going to jail was at least a small down payment on my "dues," for a lot of others it simply marked me as another crazy honky whose judgment could not be trusted. One of my black acquaintances even told me to be careful not to begin to think that I *really* knew what being in jail was like since, in his opinion (and he had served two sentences), being poor and black in jail and being white and privileged in jail were two different things.

Not getting the credit I had somehow expected for going to jail bothered me especially when I compared my relatively cool reception in Roxbury to the acclamation some other white ministers received from neighbors and parishioners in white areas. I realize of course that some ministers who participated in the Civil Rights Movement were not lauded or appreciated at all for what they did. Some even lost their jobs. Still, I had anticipated a little more appreciation from my black friends. Their matter-of-fact attitude taught me that a few days behind bars does not earn white people much capital in the ghetto where going to jail is not all that rare and not terribly noteworthy.

As my children grew up we often talked about what it meant to be in a jail. On family outings we sometimes sped past the Concord State Reformatory, a grim hulk of stone and steel a few miles from our home. Once as we drove past it my oldest daughter told me that she had gone by it the week before with another family, and the children had asked what it was. The parents had said it was where "bad people who had done bad things were locked up." She had started to cry and told them that could not possibly be true because her father had been in a jail and he was not bad and had not done any bad things. Had she been right?

I stopped the car at the next ice cream stand, bought everyone cones, and tried to answer her question as best I could. How do you translate the rudiments of ethics, civil disobedience, and modern criminology to an eight-year-old? Yes, I had broken a law and been put in jail. No, people are not just either bad or good. Everyone is a mixture of both. Yes, the reasons why people do things that get them into jail differ. No, I did not think that prison is a very good way to punish people; they only learn more tricks of the trade from other prisoners. No, I did not know what else could be done, but some judges (even then) were making people do compensatory work instead of going to jail. I explained what that meant. She nodded and munched on her strawberry softie. I sometimes overwhelm my kids when they ask a simple question. Still, I think she got the point: *bad* and *good* and *inside* and *outside* are not interchangeable terms. She learned a little bit about the questionableness of some of the moral categories we fling around. And she got an ice cream to boot.

The burglaries at our Roxbury house started in 1968, five years after we moved in and two years before we moved out. But in two years our house was burglarized nine times. We never got used to this graphic evidence of our vulnerability. It was the burglaries that made Nancy and me wonder seriously whether the people who asked us if we were forcing our own ideals on our children might be right after all. The break-ins all took place while we were away from the house, sometimes only for a couple of hours. We would return from a picnic in the park or dinner with friends to find the familiar telltale signs. A door forced open. A window broken. Inside, the house would look at first as though vandals had roamed through it: drawers opened with their contents spilled on the floor, books swept off shelves (to see what was hidden behind?) furniture upended. Then, after surveying the squalor, we would begin the search for what was missing. It was usually the same things: record players, transistors, typewriters, hair dryers, toasters—anything easy to "fence."

We always tried not to let it get to us. "Oh, well. It was an old toaster anyway," someone would say. "It wouldn't even pop up anymore." But despite our efforts to keep cheerful, it became clearer after the fifth or sixth robbery that something else was at stake. One day as we were leaving to see some friends, our younger daughter, Sarah, then aged five, came to the car dragging a tiny stove she liked to play with and the toy pots and pans that went with it. She was having a hard time carrying them all and they kept dropping on the stairs and sidewalk. I told her she did not have to bring everything along, that the children at the house we were visiting would have some toys, but she insisted. She just had to bring them, she said, because maybe if she left them the robbers would come and steal them. Shortly after that we begin looking for somewhere else to live.

We were not burglarized because we were a white family on a black block. If anything we had been luckier than our black neighbors, some of whom had been hit two or three times before we were. But I do think I know why the burglaries started, and so suddenly, after years of no such incidents at all. I did not find out until years later but the information taught me a lot about the seamy side of city life. I heard about it from a black friend who had some acquaintances in the demimonde of drugs and crime.

It seems that when the City of Boston decided to upgrade the old South End, to make it attractive to upper income "gentrification" it became necessary to push the drug-sales area out of the South End and move it somewhere else. Through that curious confraternity police have with drug dealers and vice versa, the word went out one day that, starting tomorrow, the South End was going to get hot, but that the narcotic squad would start looking the other way in the Grove Hall area.

Overnight our neighborhood became a hard drug center. And on signal the hundreds of tortured souls who frantically needed some money for a fix descended on it. Muggings, which had been a rarity on our street, started happening at three in the afternoon on clear days. Burglaries became a nightly occurrence. Black families who had lived on the block for decades and had sworn they would live there as long as they had breath, panicked and began moving out. We stuck it out for several months, hoping it was just a streak of bad luck, that it would pass. It did not. And the day Sarah came to the car with the toy stove, we called a real estate agent. The sixties—with their warmth and camaraderie and their heady sense of being part of something larger and worthwhile—ended for us, as they did for many other people, under a cloud of defeat and bewilderment. We moved away from a neighborhood we loved, feeling it had been stolen from us by forces too large for us to comprehend. I still have a hard time driving through that area, so great is my sense of outrage and loss.

It took two years after we had moved from Roxbury for us to begin to appreciate the joyful memories. We had been caught up in a dream close to the one Martin Luther King, Jr., painted at the Lincoln Memorial ("that one day *all* God's children will sit together"). The dream seemed not to have materialized. But then something else happened. We began to remember how good the simple reality, not the dream at all, had been. We remembered the winter car pools to get neighborhood kids to school events; the sledding expeditions; the church suppers; the late night meetings to fight back against the constant machinations from downtown; the beer and sandwiches in Franklin Park on lazy Sunday afternoons; the parties that started late and went later even though there was work and school in the morning; the instinct for survival that persists among black people; the capacity to keep on squeezing out the little juice that's left. These were all real, no dream. And they were black-and-white together, not "integrating," just living. So, today when I hear Aretha Franklin sing "You Make Me Feel Like a Natural Woman" or "Chain of Fools," I am glad my faith journey once took my loved ones and me to Blue Hill Avenue. It could have been no other way. If that makes me an unrealistic remnant of the sixties, so be it.

The Roxbury years: I recall them now as—how can you say it?—cozy. Even though we were a white family in a black neighborhood we felt a sense of belonging we have hardly ever felt since then. I am not romantic enough to believe that deprivation and discrimination produce a sense of community. Just as often they set people at one another's throats. What made the difference in the sixties in Roxbury was not the poverty and the prejudice but "the movement," the conviction that together we were doing something about it, that God was "on our side" and that things *would* change. We could stay up late, dance to Aretha, picket the school committee headquarters, and keep it up week after week because we all felt we were a part of something much larger than ourselves. Something

William James might have identified as "the moral equivalent of war."

More than a decade later the ardor I felt in Roxbury has been dampened but not doused. If our vision of how quickly the big picture would change was too foreshortened, it was an error of schedule not of substance. I continue to believe in the dream we fought for then not out of some stubborn unwillingness to give up an illusion but because in the battle itself we found the very community we sought. We touched and tasted a racially inclusive, sharing, struggling company of sisters and brothers. While singing we *shall* overcome, we already *had* overcome at least in part. That is something no one can ever take away.

# 9

# The Sixties and the Eighties: A Conversation with My Son

At the time of this writing my son, Martin, is twenty. He is a junior at Harvard majoring in experimental physics. I try occasionally to peruse one of his textbooks but cannot understand even the first page. He is named for Martin Luther King, Jr., with whom I worked in the Southern Christian Leadership Conference during the tumultuous days of what we then knew as the "Freedom Movement," although it has since come to be called, more modestly perhaps, just the "Civil Rights Movement." A few years back, when my son was about sixteen, we watched a TV series on King together. After the last episode, we talked more candidly than we ever had before. The conversation is reconstructed, more or less, here: a painful reminder of how quickly history moves along and how tough it is to pass on the lore and passion of one decade to another. Since this could have been a conversation that occurred in any family I call the parties **F** (father) and **S** (son).

**S** (*switching off the tube*): So you were really *there* in some of those marches and things?

**F:** Well, yes. Quite a few actually. I worked with SCLC in Selma, in Mississippi, in St. Augustine, and in Williamston, North Carolina. (*He knew, it occurs to me with a twinge of regret, that I was* away *a lot during those years. He did not know where I was.*)

**S:** Well, what was it like? I mean *really* like?

**F** (*pausing*): Well, it's hard to describe, actually. (*I feel a twitch in my stomach. This is not going to be easy. How can I describe it so he will* get *it?*) It was, well, I felt *alive* in a way I seldom have since. Like I was at the edge, where history was being made. You know what I mean? There were just a lot of us then who felt we were actually participating in history, not just watching it happen on TV. (*Can I tell him I also felt close to God, often melded bone to bone with the other people, black and white, who were marching, sitting in, demonstrating, going to jail, singing? Would he understand that part?*)

**S** (*interrupting my pause*): And you did get arrested, right?

**F:** Yes. Once with sixty other marchers in Williamston in 1963 for "parading without a permit" and violating a North Carolina Superior Court injunction not to hold that particular march. I was pretty worried that day. Parading without a permit is a minor offense, but violating a court order can carry three- to five-year prison terms. You were only two years old then and Rachel was only three and Nancy was pregnant with Sarah . . . and I did not want to go to prison.

**S:** But you *did* get put in jail?

**F:** Yeah. In the little segregated lock-up in Williamston. We all got arrested at the same time, but the jail was segregated so they put the eleven white people in one section and the forty-nine blacks in another.

**S:** Were you scared?

**F:** The truth is I was a lot scareder just *before* the march from the little black church where it started than I was in the jail itself. A sympathetic white preacher in the town had told us the night before that a lot of the local white folks were planning to stand along the march route with clubs and chains and that the local police had said they could not "guarantee our safety" as they put it. But there was also a rumor that the state police were on the way and that they were under orders to protect us until we got into the jail. We weren't sure though. We sang a lot, songs like "Do You Want Your Freedom?" and some of the black people prayed out loud the whole time.

**S:** How about you? Did you pray?

**F:** Well, yeah. I did. But inside. Outside I tried to look brave. The thing that bothered me most was not *my* dying, but how much I would miss you and the family. It was hard not to find some good reason to sneak away before we started. What kept me in the line I think was a fifteen-year-old black kid next to me who told me he had been in four marches like this already. I don't know. Somehow I could not let him go without me or admit to myself that I was a chicken.

**S:** Did you get beat up?

**F:** No, pushed and shoved a bit by the cops when they arrested us but not beat up. Actually the cops seemed as glad as we were to get us and themselves inside the jail, away from that crowd.

**S:** Oh, the crowd really came then? With clubs and stuff?

**F:** They were there all right. How much hardware they were carrying was hard to see since I was staring straight ahead of me and the state police (*they had in fact arrived in time*) were lining the march route. I guess someone had told them not to let North Carolina get a bad name. It was supposed to be "better," whatever that means, than places like Mississippi and Alabama. Anyway I admit I was glad to see those uniforms. I don't like any kind of pain and I sure was not up for martyrdom.

**S:** "Martyrdom?" What do you mean?

**F** (*thinking, God how I have neglected this kid's religious education!*): Martyrdom. Being a martyr. Someone who willingly dies for what he believes in.

**S:** Oh, yeah.

**F** (*thinking*): (*Does he? Do I? Was I ready, if not willing that day in Williamston to die for something? Or was I still riding on the adolescent illusion that had gotten me through the North Sea mine fields? What* *would I die for, willingly today? I mean today? If someone offered a guaranteed deal, would I die today to prevent nuclear war? Can anyone claim to have anything like a mature faith who is not ready to give his or her own life for something?*)

**S** (*noticing I have temporarily left the conversation*): Dad?

**F:** Uh, yeah?

**S:** Did you think it did any *good*, I mean all that marching and . . .

**F** (*torn between wanting to tell him whether it did any good did not matter because we did what was right, whether it made a difference or not, and not wanting to look like a dummy who risked getting clobbered for no net result*): Well, yeah. It made *some* difference, but it did not do all we hoped it would.

**S:** What do you mean?

**F:** Well, people are still not equal in this country. We still have racism. Look at how many more people of color are poor, in jail. . . .

**S** (*shouting at his sister in the next room*): Half this popcorn is burned. (*Voice from next room*): Then make it yourself next time, dumbo!

**F** (*shifting ground slightly since Martin has heard my equality rap before and is not moved to high emotion by it now*): Also some people think Martin Luther King was only beginning to see the real problem just before he died and that racism goes deeper and is tied up with our economic system, and . . .

**S:** That's what Malcolm X was talking about, wasn't it?

**F:** Yeah, how did you know?

**S:** You told me once. The time you told me about that guy you met in the bar in Roxbury with Bill Stevens, the guy who used to burglarize those parties on Beacon Hill with Malcolm X. When we watched that other TV show.

**F:** Yeah. The bartender was this *huge* guy named Big John, about six foot seven and three hundred pounds. When I walked in that bar with Bill he said, "Stevens, why don't you take your *Caucasian* friend somewhere else!" I looked toward the door, but Bill said, "Hey, no, Big John. This guy wants to hear about Malcolm." So Big John sized me up, pursed his gigantic lips, then pointed to a bar stool and poured out three absolutely *huge* glasses of whiskey. (*I show how big the glasses were with my hands, exaggerating slightly.*) "Malcolm," Big John said, nodding his head, "Malcolm, now there was a *man*. Why Malcom could get on the subway at Dudley Station and by the time he got to Park Street he'd have four guys he never met talked into doing a job on the Hill. There was a *man*. Why . . ."

**S:** Yeah, Dad. You told me that one before too, and Big John was in the same jail with Malcolm, right?

**F:** You remember.

**S:** But Big John did not become a Muslim like Malcolm did because when he found out he'd have to stop playing poker and eating pork chops and drinking booze, he said, "Shit, I'd rather just stay a Baptist." Right?

**F:** Okay. You've heard me tell that before.

**S:** More than once.

**F:** Well, it's still pretty good. Anyway, Big John went on for an hour about Malcolm during his Boston days when they called him "Detroit Red."

**S:** And you just sat there and *listened*? (*Implying I don't do that much?*)

**F:** I sure did. I thought I was listening to one of the original twelve disciples talk about Jesus Christ. I mean not what Malcolm X *did* but the impact he had on the people he met. I wasn't surprised though. I'd heard Malcolm X speak at the Law School Forum a couple of years before and I've never seen an audience so knocked over by anyone. And that was a white audience. He was the best orator I have ever heard, including King himself.

**S:** Then why didn't you name me Malcolm instead of Martin?

**F:** Martin, you have to understand that even in the sixties there were limits to what nice white liberal people could do, or even *think*. Besides I still believe King's nonviolence made him the greater of the two, I mean in the long, long run. Malcolm was flashy, fiery, eloquent. All that. But King knew that the human species has to evolve other ways of doing things than war and violence . . . otherwise the species will not survive. He said that over and over and . . .

**S:** Want to watch the news?

**F:** No. Not particularly. Thinking about the sixties makes me nostalgic. It was such a great time, and there we were in Roxbury right in the middle of the action.

**S:** *And* the burglaries *and* the riots *and* the garbage *and* those fire engines that came by every night with their bells clanging.

**F** (*a little touchy*): Well, where the hell did you want to spend the first eight years of your life? In some snooty suburb? You got street-wise at seven while most white kids your age were getting off on Romper Room.

**S:** Oh, come on. Don't make a big deal out of it! So what? So we lived in a black slum. So what. Besides I did *not* get street-wise. All I learned was how to size up how big a kid was and how to slip out of sight and how to run fast.

**F:** That's what I mean. Street-wise. And it was *not* a slum. It was a working class black neighborhood.

**S:** Yeah. Working class. And what kind of work did those women in the apartment house next door do? Where the shooting happened that night, and the cops and the ambulance came and everybody was in the street?

**F:** You were supposed to be too young to know what was going on in there.

**S:** Maybe I was street-wiser than you *thought* I was.

**F:** No, seriously. Do you think it—like, *impaired* you or anything that we lived in a black neighborhood when you were a kid? Do you wish we had lived somewhere else?

**S** (*thinking*): No. (*Pause. Popcorn munching*) Do you think there'll be another time like the sixties, Dad?

**F** (*also thinking*): No. Not with everything we had going then. But there'll be something like it, and it could happen soon. Maybe the nuclear disarmament movement will be the freedom movement of the eighties. I hope so.

**S** (*seems to be thinking intensely for the first time in the conversation*): But what if we don't do any better on that one than you guys did on the freedom movement or the Civil Rights Movement or whatever it was? Then what?

**F** (*I have no answer. I say nothing.*)

**S:** I mean, trying to get it so people can *vote* is one thing. Even if some of them still can't vote when you're done, it isn't the end of the world. You can keep trying. But if a nuclear war happens, kapow! All over.

**F:** Do you think about that very often!

**S:** Yeah! (*a little angry*) Do you think I'll ever be sitting talking with *my* kids about the good old days of the anti-nuclear war marches and all that stuff? You guys had it easy then by comparison. You had some fat sheriffs to deal with like the one we just saw on TV. What was his name?

**F:** Bull Connor

**S:** And you even had a lot of the courts behind you. I think you exaggerate what a big deal it was. I know a couple of people got killed, like your friend in Selma. What was his name?

**F:** Jim Reeb, but there were lots of others.

**S:** Okay, I'm sorry. But don't you see how much harder this is going to be for us. I mean, God! The Pentagon, the Kremlin, where do you start? You guys at least knew where to *start*!

**F** (*knowing Martin has already been to a couple of demonstrations*): Well, you've already started, like the time we went to the vigil in New London against the nuclear-armed submarine, and . . .

**S:** But, Dad, nothing is happening. They are still making those things. They *ignored* us. We froze our behinds walking up and down. Okay, we had a good time, with the people from the church there and all. But *they ignored* us.

**F** (*realizing I do* not *have much to say*): Well, they can't ignore us forever. If *enough people see what's at stake and just refuse to permit the* thing to go on . . . (*I peter out*).

**S:** Is there time?

**F** (*realizing this is the most profound question he has asked and that he means it*): I think there is (*Do I mean it?*) I think we will turn back from it. If the missiles are not in the air at this moment, then we have time. I can't believe God would permit human beings to wipe out our own species. It's just too unthinkable.

**S:** What does God have to do with it? (*He is not being snide. He is really asking. He does not usually like to get into what theologians call "God talk" but this time he is asking.*)

**F** (*wishing I had a better, clearer, more convincing answer*): I don't know. Only for me *God* means there is always that unpredictable unforeseen, surprising—(*I am stumbling and rambling*) . . . that things we cannot predict or plan for happen. God means a lot of other things too, but when I get in a gloomy mood about all this, it comes down to my still believing that somehow, somewhere, something will break in. I don't know what it will be but I have this hunch, this hope. Otherwise . . .

**S:** Otherwise what?

**F** (*a long pause*): Otherwise I guess I'd just give up.

**S** (*says nothing*).

**F:** Do you think about this often?

**S:** You already asked me that. I told you, yes I do.

**F:** Does it make it hard to study, to get ready for some future that . . . well, you know . . . may not come?

**S:** What else can you do?

**F** (*silent. I see he is going to say something else*).

**S:** I guess I have the same . . . like . . . hope. That something will turn up. Something will change. People will see what's happening. What else can you do?

**F:** Yeah, what else *can* you do?

**S** (*pause*): Want to watch the late movie on 38? It's *Godzilla's Return*. You know. It's that crazy monster that comes up out of the sea . . . in Japan I think . . . and smashes all the telephone poles. But it is so fake, Dad, really so *fake*. You can almost see where it's been screwed together. It's so *funny*. Wanna' watch?

**F:** (*thinking, what a courageous kid you are and what a terrible world we have created for you. God bless you, my son. I hope you do better with the eighties than we did with the sixties*): Okay, Martin. Let's watch *Godzilla*. We're out of popcorn, though. This time why don't we make it ourselves.

# 10
# Latins and Liberation

Latin America and its theology have played an important role both in my theology and in my faith journey. In this chapter, inspired perhaps by the Latin American penchant for irony, I have chosen to describe that role in the form of an interview with myself as both interviewer and interviewee.

**Int:** How did the "Latin Connection" get started?

**Me:** In the summer of 1968 I was living in Cuernavaca, Mexico, and teaching at CIDOC, the Center for Intercultural Documentation which was then led by Ivan Illich. I had more or less fled there to get away from a U.S. that seemed to be going to pieces. Martin Luther King, Jr., had been assassinated in April. Then in June, Bobby Kennedy for whom I had been working in California was also shot. I decided it was time to accept a long-standing invitation from Ivan to go to Cuernavaca, teach a little at his Center, and also learn Spanish.

One of the people I met at CIDOC was Monsignor Sergio Mendez-Arceo, the bishop of Cuernavaca. Another was Francisco Juliaño, the famous lay preacher and organizer of the peasant leagues in Northeast Brazil who was in political exile. Both of them gave me some feeling for the underlying ferment out of which the new theological currents were emerging. Then one day I met a guy who was carrying a manuscript written by a Brazilian theologian named Rubem Alves. It seemed to be written from a distinctly Latin American point of view. I was excited by it, and started looking for a publisher. Finally we got one to take the risk, and I wrote the preface. So far as I know it is the first Latin American liberation theology book to be published in the U.S.

**Int:** Isn't it ironical that this first-of-its-kind book is written by a Presbyterian, not by a Catholic?

**Me:** That just shows what a refined sense of humor God has! Imagine, a *Brazilian* Calvinist! It's almost a contradiction in terms. And yet, liberation theology is by its very essence a theology of the margin. It comes from the edge, the periphery of the empire. Maybe a Brazilian Protestant is even more on the margin. Still, as one of my Latin friends says, "Everyone in Latin America is a Catholic, even the Protestants." The book could not have arisen in any other context. That is what makes it liberation theology: its radically contextual character.

**Int:** How did your involvement in Latin America and in the liberation theology movement continue?

**Me:** Well, one of my books, a little one I wrote for a Baptist student conference in 1963 entitled *God's Revolution and Man's Responsibility* (I was still using the generic *man* then) was translated into Spanish under the title *El Cristo Como Rebelde* (Christ as a Rebel). It was widely read in Latin America, and I began to get inquiries about visiting there. That was in part why I went to Cuernavaca, to learn Spanish.

**Int:** So you went back again?

**Me:** Time and time again.

**Int:** Didn't you come close to getting into real trouble once in Mexico?

**Me:** It was close, but I'm still not sure how serious the trouble would have been.

**Int:** Well, what happened?

**Me:** It was in 1969. I had gone to Mexico City as a consultant for a meeting sponsored by the Latin American (Roman Catholic) Bishops on the problem of North American mass media "invasion." Juan Luis Segundo a Jesuit from Uruguay was also there. Remember this was just a year after the shooting of the student demonstrators in Mexico City at the Plaza of the Three Cultures. The city was still a little jumpy. One afternoon, after our conference had been going about three days, a crowd of right-wing Catholic high school students swarmed into the hotel carrying sticks and placards. They tried to interrupt the proceedings, and although they looked young, no one was sure why they were carrying those sticks. Somebody thought they were looking for Segundo and me; so the chairman of the conference quietly suggested we slip out a side door before they found out which ones we were (there were no name tags). I thought the precaution was a little silly, but later a Mexican friend told me that in those days the police and right-wing groups often conspired to get a scuffle going and that this looked like it might have been a setup. The way it worked was that a group like the "Falcons" or some other right-wing cadre would start a melee and then the police would move in and beat up the people the Falcons were attacking. In any case, I did not question the wisdom of the chairman. Two Mexican friends took Segundo and me out the back door and down the street where we sat for a couple of hours in the backroom of the only kosher restaurant-and-delicatessen in Mexico City. Symbolic, eh?

**Int:** Symbolic of what?

**Me:** Well, I don't know. Anyway, the young mob finally left without causing any fracas. It seemed they were put up to it by a priest who believed all the propaganda about the Communists taking over the church. One of the conference participants told me he thought the priest had gotten his information from the American embassy. At the time I thought that sounded a little farfetched, but nowadays I am not so sure. Every American embassy in Latin America has a CIA person on the staff. And they spend their time guiding, influencing, and financing political groups. I am not sure, even today, who put those kids up to the invasion of the hotel. They were obviously not very well informed themselves. Nor am I sure what they wanted to happen. Still, in retrospect, especially after the horrible raid the Falcons pulled off in Mexico City a few months later—in which dozens of people were killed—I was just as glad to be eating cheeze blintzes with Segundo at the time rather than finding out what would have happened if . . .

**Int:** Did that incident make you apprehensive about going back to Latin America?

**Me:** Maybe it should have. It didn't. My next trip was made in response to an invitation from the Pontifical Catholic University of Peru, from the theological faculty where Gustavo Guttiérez teaches.

**Int:** He is the "father" of liberation theology?

**Me:** I guess you could say that. At least he published the first book out of Latin America with the word *liberation* in the title.

**Int:** What did you do in Peru?

**Me:** Well, I hung out with the Maryknollers, visited missions in the favellas, and became the first Protestant theologian ever to lecture at the university. At that time my Spanish was still very weak. I had prepared my lectures in Spanish but only gave one. Then my hosts pled with me to give the rest in English and they would provide an interpreter! So I did.

**Int:** Did you go anywhere on that trip?

**Me:** Yes, I visited Chile, Argentine, and Brazil. In Chile I was a guest of the Centro Bellarmino where Father Vekemans who later became one of the principal critics of liberation theology was still holding the fort. I was there during the campaign that resulted in the election of Salvador Allende as president. The staff of the Centro was split over the election but most of them opposed llende and supported the Christian Democrats. A couple supported Allende and the Popular Unity coalition. Later on I discovered that the Centro Bellarmino was more or less a think tank for the Christian Democrats, so I am surprised any Allende supporters were there at all.

On the way home I spent Holy Week in Brazil, part of it with

Dom Helder Camara in Recife. He invited me to meet his staff in the diocesan headquarters, where he holds his very informal interviews with people. It is an amazing place, swarming with people who want to see him and ask for a favor. Pigs and chickens wander around in the corridors. Babies cry. Donkeys bellow on the porch.

**Int:** What did you talk about?

**Me:** Mostly Dom Helder wanted me to talk with his people about Christian attitudes toward violence and nonviolence. He is strongly committed to a nonviolent approach to revolution in Brazil.

**Int:** What did you say?

**Me:** I had a hard time saying anything. It was shortly after Dom Helder's own secretary, a young priest, had been murdered by a right-wing death squad. Dom Helder put it in graphic terms. He had no fear for his own life, he said. He thought that as a bishop he was relatively safe. But whenever he spoke out against oppression, his enemies took it out on one of his priests. I finally told him and his staff that I had no advice at all for them, that it would be utterly pretentious for me to say anything one way or another about violence when I was about to return to the safety of the U.S.A. and they would have to stay and live in the situation.

**Int:** Back to liberation theology, what was your next "Latin connection"?

**Me:** Well, in 1973 I received a letter from Augusto Cotto, a Baptist minister from El Salvador, a "product" (as they say) of American Baptist missionary work there. Augusto was then living in Mexico and serving as rector of the Baptist Seminary in Mexico City, which has students from Central America and the Caribbean as well as Mexico. Augusto invited me to teach for a semester at the seminary. I had a sabbatical leave from Harvard coming up the next year, so I said yes. Ever since then, the Seminario Bautista de Mexico has been my principal home-away-from-home in Latin America. Significantly, the first night I arrived to teach in 1974, Gustavo Guttiérez was staying there and we talked until 2:00 A.M. The seminario is a meeting point for engaged Christians from all over Latin America.

**Int:** But something happened to Cotto?

**Me:** Sadly, yes. In 1979 he began returning as often as he could to El Salvador to keep up his contacts with the Christian churches there. He was openly sympathetic with the opposition. One day the small plane in which he was being flown mysteriously crashed near the coast of his country. Some people suspect foul play. I do not know. In any case, he is dead now, one of the thousands who have died since the civil war in El Salvador started. He left a young wife and three small children. Augusto is one of the reasons why I feel such a personal stake in Central America.

**Int:** But did you actually teach liberation theology in Mexico? Isn't that like carrying coals to Newcastle?

**Me:** It is hard to believe, but many Latin American seminarians did not know much about the theology that is coming out of their own countries. Both Protestant and Catholic seminarians have been fed for decades on theologies imported from Europe and North America. The students in the Baptist seminary itself were much better off. Their faculty members were in touch with Latin American currents. But the students from the other seminaries who came into my classes through cross-registration had to hear about Latin American theology, ironically, from a *gringo*.

**Int:** You've also spent some time in southern Mexico, right?

**Me:** Yes. In 1977 I met Samuel Ruis who is bishop of San Cristobal de las Casas in the state of Chiapas on the border of Guatemala. Chiapas has a large population of Indians, indigenes. Bishop Ruis has become their champion against all the interests, including Pemex the Mexican national petroleum company, which are intent on ripping them off.

**Int:** But is Ruis also interesting theologically?

**Me:** Ruis is an example of how liberation theology can transform a whole region. In the many years he has been bishop there he has trained thousands of indigenous catechists who are elected by their own villages and then ordained as deacons. They have worked out a fabulous catechism that combines Indian creation myths, the Exodus story, and a heavy emphasis on "Jesus Christ the liberator." Ruis proves that liberation theology is not an intellectual pastime. His ministry has probably assured the cultural, and maybe even the physical survival of thousands and thousands of *indigenes.* I believe that liberation theology is *pastoral* theology. Some critics of liberation theology claim it has no pastoral dimension: they say it cannot inform counseling or religious education; they should see what is happening in Chiapas. Under Bishop Ruis liberation theology *is* pastoral theology *par excellence.*

**Int:** But is that the only place?

**Me:** Heavens, no! The entire "grass-roots Christian community" movement in Brazil and elsewhere is an expression, may be even the social basis for liberation theology. It is only North American and European critics who claim liberation theology is the product of elites and high intellectual strata. No one who knows the Latin American scene could possibly say that.

**Int:** What was the joke about your teaching in the seminary in Chiapas? I did not quite get it before.

**Me:** Neither did I at first. Bishop Ruis told me in Mexico City he would like me to "visit the seminary" and spend some time speaking with his seminarians. I thought that would be great. Then, when I got to San Cristobal, the bishop took me out to dinner with some of his staff. One of them was the rector of the seminary. Again he reminded me that I had agreed to "visit the seminary" and I said I was looking forward to that. He started to laugh uproariously and so did the seminary rector. Then he told me that he had *closed* the seminary several years before and that his seminarians were all scattered in small villages throughout Chiapas. They were being prepared for the priesthood by working alongside older priests, missionaries, political organizers, health workers, indigenous catechists, and so on. Every few weeks the seminarians from a particular area came together for a few days somewhere to discuss their reading, hear a lecture, talk about the work they were doing and get their assignments. So the joke was that in order to "visit the seminary" I would have to travel by four-wheel-drive jeep through some of the roughest terrain anywhere in Mexico. That was what he thought was so funny. For me it was a treat. I got out into the wildest country I have ever seen, between San Cristobal and Villahermosa. It is sparsely settled, mostly Indians, but it is rich in oil so it's hotly contested turf. In a little village called Bacharón, which you will not find on most maps, I spent a few days with a cluster of the bishop's seminarians. It was great. I lectured in the morning and held a discussion with them. In the evening we sat by a fire and discussed what they were doing, sang songs and drank rum and Coke. Altogether it provided me with an insight into what "theological education" means in a setting of poverty and struggle.

**Int:** Then what?

**Me:** I knew that the meeting of the Latin American bishops originally scheduled for the fall of 1978 would be a critical one. The previous such gathering, held ten years before in Medellin, Colombia, had turned out to be a kind of watershed. It was there the bishops explicitly enunciated the church's "preferential option for the poor" and identified imperialism and economic dependency as the enemies of justice on their continent. I knew there were lots of people who wanted to use the next meeting—to take place in Puebla, Mexico—to slow down or stop this so-called "progressive" thrust in the church. Some bishops, and some stringpullers in Rome, wanted to strangle the Christian-base communities and stifle liberation theology with some kind of warning or even an official condemnation. I wanted very badly to be present at the conference of the bishops in Puebla, so I got myself declared the official press representative of *Commonweal,* the liberal Catholic weekly and of *Christianity and Crisis,* the bimonthly on whose editorial board I serve. I became a *"periodista"!*

**Int:** But why could you not go as an official observer?

**Me:** The conservative faction that got control of the planning process for Puebla made sure the number of observers who were allowed to attend was strictly limited. They were *very* few. This faction also made sure the best-known liberation theologians were not invited, that the most progressive bishops were not there (Mendez-Arceo and Ruis, for example were not invited), and that some highly respectable Catholic journalists, like Gary Macoin, were barred from the proceedings.

**Int:** But you did go?

**Me:** Eventually, yes. I was there for the entire meeting, and I wrote accounts of it for *Commonweal* and *Christianity and Crisis*. I wrote the one for *C and C*, incidentally, with Faith Sand who is on the staff of *Missiology* magazine, published out of Fuller Seminary. She is a well-known evangelical journalist, and I enjoyed appearing in print co-authoring something with someone from Fuller.

**Int:** Why?

**Me:** It forces people to see that the Christian movment in Latin America breaks our established categories of "liberal," and "conservative," and so forth. Many Latin American Protestant evangelicals are far too politically radical for their North American compatriots, but at the same time their theology seems retarded to academic liberals. Liberation theology turns a lot of things on their heads that way.

**Int:** Wasn't that the meeting Pope John Paul II addressed?

**Me:** Yes, it was his first trip abroad after becoming pope in February 1979.

**Int:** What interest did Puebla have in liberation theology?

**Me:** It was the hot topic there, along with Christian-base communities. Although the best-known liberation theologians were not invited and the conference itself was stacked with curial imports, the bishops who were sympathetic to the "option for the poor" and the base communities won the day. The document expresses strong support both for the church's special responsibility for the poor and for the validity of the base communities.

**Int:** Even though the liberation theologians were not there?

**Me:** Well, they were not *officially* there. But many of them came on their own, informally and unofficially, and made themselves available to any of the bishops who wanted to

consult with them. It was a funny scene. Many of the
theologians were living in a seedy little hotel called the "San
Francisco" several blocks off the main plaza. It was selected, I
think, because it was inexpensive and inobvious. But the
people who picked it out did not know that it was alleged to be
one of the main hotels in Puebla used by the prostitutes. This
became a joke. Bishops sneaked into the "San Francisco" at
1:00 A.M. to consult with theologians about the fourth or fifth
draft of some section of the Puebla document and then left in a
couple of hours. The front desk people never batted an
eyelash. They were used to a lot of nocturnal comings and
goings!

**Int:** Did you talk with the theologians at the "San Francisco"?

**Me:** Yes, quite a bit, especially with Jon Sobrino who was
concentrating on the more "theological" sections and with
Xabier Gorostiaga who was pouring over the economic justice
sections. Xabier is now working in the economic planning
division of the Sandinista government in Nicaragua.

**Int:** Did you influence the document yourself?

**Me:** Not at all. By then my Spanish was good enough to
lecture and read but it was not up to entering into late night
machinations over the various drafts of documents. Besides, I
felt in some ways I should respect my *periodista* status.
Journalists, they say, are supposed to report the news, not
make it.

**Int:** Did anyone think it odd that you were there as a
journalist?

**Me:** Not really, since a lot of other theologians had used the
same ruse, seeing that the "observer" status was so hard to get.
Only one time did it become awkward, and even then it turned
out okay. I went to the grandiose cocktail party the bishops
gave for the journalists. Hundreds of people were present—
three journalists for every bishop at Puebla, someone told me,
and I believe it. Anyway, at the cocktail party I met Monsignor
Lopez Trujillo who was then the general-secretary of the whole
Latin American Bishops' Conference and has now become the
president. Lopez Trujillo was viewed by many of the

liberationists as the main villain, the arch-enemy of what Medellin had stood for. Every journalist there wanted to interview him, but he granted no interviews at all. That evening I met him. He raised his eyebrows when he saw my name on my badge. And then he shook his head. "You're not *really* a journalist, are you?" he asked. I blushed a bit, as though my cover had been blown, and explained why I was wearing a *periodista* ID. He had read two of my books, he said, and asked me if we could leave the party and have supper together.

**Int:** Did that surprise you?

**Me:** I was stunned. But even more stunned, and a little miffed, were the authentic journalists who overheard the conversation and the invitation and wondered why I was getting a privilege they were not.

**Int:** Well, why were you?

**Me:** Lopez Trujillo did not want to be interviewed. He wanted to talk, and he wanted to talk to someone other than all the bishops and theologians he had been talking with for days. He is an intelligent man. I think he was looking for some theological dinner conversation, and although he knew we would not agree on many things, he thought it would be interesting.

**Int:** Was it?

**Me:** Indeed. Lopez Trujillo reminds me very much of the North American "neo-conservatives" like Daniel Bell and Peter Berger. He sees religion as a part of culture, sustaining and nourishing people in difficult times. He thinks Latin America is in the midst of chaotic upheaval and he wants traditional religion to remain, as it were, above the fray. So he opposes the liberation theology movement even though he sometimes uses its language. Still, I think he is a worthy opponent, a thoughtful man, though some Latin American Christians think he is unscrupulous. What my long dinner conversation taught me is that in Latin America the ideas associated with liberation theology can never be evaluated merely on the level of ideas. All ideas have consequences, and Lopez Trujillo knows this very well.

**Int:** So what was the overall effect of Puebla on liberation theology?

**Me:** I am tempted to answer that the way I heard Gustavo Guttiérez answer it just after Puebla. It doesn't really matter what happens to liberation *theology* he said; it is what happens to *liberation* that counts.

**Int:** But that doesn't go together too well with what you just said about ideas having consequences.

**Me:** Right, so I would not put it that way exactly. What happened at Puebla was not only that liberation theology was not condemned, although that is significant. What happened is that it was *confirmed*. Puebla proved that Medellin was not just a fluke. Not that the whole Catholic church in Latin America has suddenly gone liberationist. Not at all. But it is true to say that within the church an epochal movement, theologically and institutionally, is underway. Brazil is now the largest Catholic country in the world. And the demographic center of Catholic Christianity has now shifted to Latin America. In one sense, Latin America holds the future of the Catholic Church within its future. This explains in part why so much of Catholic social teaching and missionary emphasis has shifted so dramatically to the Third World, to questions of global justice.

**Int:** Some newspaper here in the USA reported that Pope John Paul II condemned liberation theology in Mexico.

**Me:** That's not true. He did not. It seems a reporter who does not speak French misunderstood something the pope said in French and put his misunderstanding on the wire. Later, when the pope got back to Rome and heard about that report he issued a statement explicitly denying that any such condemnation had ever been made. The misquotation was widely reported. The pope's denial was not. Many people *wanted* to hear such a condemnation; that may explain why some newspapers seized on it. There was even a demonstration in Puebla by conservative Mexican business groups. I have a snapshot of them marching in the street carrying what has to be one of the strangest placards I have ever seen. It says, "Liberation Theology is Bad for Business"!

**Int:** Where did you go after Puebla?

**Me:** I returned to Mexico City and taught the rest of the semester at the Seminario Bautista. I also participated in a weekly seminar with Protestant and Catholic theologians; we studied Puebla, the pope's visit, and the impact of the whole thing on Latin America, especially Mexico.

**Int:** Did you come to any conclusions?

**Me:** For one, the Mexican government was scared out of its pants by the pope's visit. They had not expected anything like that sort of reception. He turned out larger crowds than anyone in Mexican history, ever. I think they began to get nightmares about some radical Catholic take-over. There were even reports—one was published in *Excelsior* the leading Mexico City daily—that the CIA had been ordered to infiltrate and monitor Christian movements in Latin America to be on the lookout for any such development. I got pretty sore about this. Together with several other U.S. citizens who were living at the time in Mexico I sent a letter of protest to my fellow Baptist Jimmy Carter, who was president then, asking him how he would like to have a spy in his Sunday school class.

The main conclusion we came to, however, is that even in officially secularized Mexico there is an enormous deposit of popular Christian belief and sentiment, and that it could be a source of motivation for significant change.

**Int:** In Mexico?

**Me:** Everywhere in Latin America, but I still hold the opinion—not held by many others—that Mexico is in some ways the key to the whole continent. Paradoxically that is because of the very factors that once gave rise to the pathetic little self-deprecating slogan you often hear in Mexico, "Pobrecito Mexico, tan lejos de diós, tan cerca de los estado unidos!"

**Int:** Which means . . ?

**Me:** "Poor little Mexico, so far from God, so close to the United States!" But you see that is just the point. It is Mexico's closeness to the U.S., and its humiliating defeat by the U.S. in a war, that has been the principal factor inhibiting any significant movement toward justice there. Mexico still has an appallingly bad income and wealth distribution picture. Enormous affluence cohabits with obscene poverty. The restaurants and night clubs of the Zona Rosa glitter away only a couple miles from the vast, stinking slum of Netzahualcoyotyl, one of the largest and most despair-filled slums I have ever seen anywhere. "Neza," where one of my best friends in Mexico, a Benedictine named Alex Morell, worked, does not appear on any official map of Mexico, by the way, even though it is larger than Boston. They just don't want you to know it is there.

**Int:** So Mexico is more important then, say, Brazil or Argentina?

**Me:** Who's to say, really? But if Mexico could begin to feel itself closer to God and a little more independent of the U.S., anything could happen.

**Int:** What about liberation theology in Central America?

**Me:** I visited Nicaragua in 1981 when I lectured at the Baptist Seminary in Managua and at the Valdivieso Ecumenical Center. I was impressed. Nicaragua has already set an example of a revolution in which most democratic freedoms are preserved while basic structural changes are made and the people themselves are drawn into the political process. I think the Christians in Nicaragua are playing an absolutely vital role. That marks a turning point in the history of modern revolutionary movements. This is the first time the Christians were on the people's side from the beginning. Nicaragua will change both Christianity and the revolutionary process itself. It is bound to.

**Int:** Any last thoughts, maybe, on the future of liberation theology?

**Me:** Liberation theology is growing up. In Nicaragua, for example, theologians have to deal not just with how to get a dictator out, but with what you do when you get into power. How you make tough decisions. Now people need more than stirring songs and slogans, though I suppose those will always have a role. Now liberation theology has to develop a social ethic for *ruling*. Also, liberation theology needs, desperately, I think, a real *ecclesiology*, a way to think about the church itself as a factor in the whole picture. In Latin America, and elsewhere, Christians have been better at telling others about justice and democracy and equality. Now some of the critique has to be directed at the churches themselves. The Christian-base community movement is already doing some of that.

**Int:** You hear a lot about these so-called "base communities" nowadays but I am not at all sure I know what they are.

**Me:** You are not alone. The term is used very loosely. When someone is being more careful, however, it refers to the rapidly proliferating small Christian study-worship-and-action groups all over Latin America but especially in Brazil where some people claim there are between forty and ninety thousand of them. What they represent is a transformation of the church not only in its theology (though that is happening also) but also in its form of social organization. Instead of the hierarchical, pyramidal, top-to-bottom structure which was introduced at the time of the Spanish *conquista* and has continued throughout nearly four centuries, the Christian-base communities represent a participatory, lay-led, more equalitarian style of corporate Christian existence.

**Int:** How did they get started?

**Me:** There are differences of opinion about that. Some people believe there have always been something like Christian-base communities in the crevices and interstices of church life in Latin America, that they have just come out in the open and blossomed.

**Int:** What's the other opinion?

**Me:** That they go back to the late fifties and early sixties when the Catholic hierarchy in Latin America, along with the Vatican, got concerned about the growth of Protestantism and of the various more-or-less socialistically inclined workers and peasants movements on the continent.

**Int:** Was there any real reason for that concern, or was it paranoia?

**Me:** It was not just paranoia, at least as far as the Protestant groups are concerned. In Chile, for example, at that time the Pentecostal movement was spreading like wildfire. Some Chilean scholars predicted that at the growth rates then current, Chile would have a Pentecostal majority by 1985. From the Catholic point of view this was not a happy prospect. Part of the problem, they thought, was that there were not enough priests to go around. So they started, in Chile and elsewhere, to train lay people to lead services—except for the Mass itself—and to lead study groups. When the lay people got the hang of it, they began to shape the *communidades de base* in ways the hierarchy had not expected. They also, incidentally, left behind a lot of their anti-protestant tilt. Many of them are ecumenically inclusive today.

**Int:** And what about the threat of socialist trade unions and peasant leagues?

**Me:** Well, that was a real challenge too, but only in terms of a static conception of Catholic social teaching, one which holds to the incompatability of Christianity and socialism. Hardly anyone holds that view in Latin America anymore.

**Int:** Hardly *anyone?*

**Me:** Well, that's an exaggeration. Let's say it would be hard to find a respectable theologian anywhere on the continent who would defend the incompatability of Christianity and social-ism. More important, the official statements of the bishops and of the pope himself—especially his encyclical On Human Work, suggest that there is no necessary conflict at all. If anything, the official pronouncements seem to make it more difficult to be a capitalist and a Christian in some respects.

**Int:** So the base communities may have started as a way of combating Protestantism and socialism and have become in fact the very places where both tendencies have made their way into the church?

**Me:** No, I would not put it that way, though some people do. These base communities should *not* be confused with some "protestantizing" tendency. Protestant congregations in Latin America are often just as badly preacher-dominated as the ones we have here. Sometimes worse. They are rarely participatory or equalitarian. Also they tend to be somewhat otherworldly. Again, with some important exceptions, many local Protestant congregations in Latin America divert people from the political process while the base communities tend to propel people into it. These base communities are the form Catholic Christianity is taking as it begins, at long last, really to indigenize itself into a culture it was imposed on top of for so many years.

**Int:** And base communities as "openings to the left"?

**Me:** Again you have to realize that in Latin America, very few people associate socialism with atheistic, totalitarian tyranny. They utilize marxist tools of analysis, things like the idea of class conflict, the role of foreign capital in perpetuating poverty, the essential role of the poor in gaining their own liberation, and so forth. The liberation of Latin America is not a battle to impose some theoretical system. It is directed toward getting rid of the stranglehold the giant international corporations and the domestic elites now hold. By and large, politically aware Latin Americans are not very impressed with "isms." They are taken up with concrete historical tasks.

**Int:** What tasks?

**Me:** You keep pressing don't you? Many reflective Christians in Latin America describe the task as "accompanying the poor in *their* historical project."

**Int:** Doesn't that romanticize "the poor" a bit?

**Me:** I don't think so. What it does is to express in practical terms what Dussel and Guttiérez and others have said about the historic role of the poor in the light of biblical theology, that is, to be the intermediaries between earthly history and the kingdom of God. This is probably the key insight of liberation theology, comparable to Luther's rediscovery of justification by faith.

**Int:** The theological significance of the poor?

**Me:** Exactly. And when you study the biblical record with this in mind, you can only be amazed that this teaching has been ignored or covered up for so long. The special, privileged place of the poor—the broken-hearted, the fatherless, the

widows—in God's purpose is so glaringly evident throughout
the whole of scriptural history, it is amazing that it has been
successfully fuzzed over for so long.

**Int:** I am going to press a little harder.

**Me:** Press on!

**Int:** What is this business of the poor, or anyone else for that
matter, being the *mediator* between history and the kingdom?
Doesn't some classical theology insist that only Jesus Chri⌐⌐ is
the mediator, that we do not need another one?

**Me:** Yes. But Catholic theology, and some forms of
Protestant theology, have also been interested in the question
of *how* Christ, as savior or Liberator, is *actually present* in human
history. Even Lutheran theology, which opposes any media-
tional view most consistently and tries to keep the "two
kingdoms" as separate as possible, still has to deal with this
somehow. It usually comes down to Christ's being present in
the proclamation of the Word. Catholic theology has always
had a more corporate, more embodied view of mediation. The
poor, from this point of view, do not mediate the Kingdom
because they are somehow nicer or more virtuous or smarter
or anything like that. God has chosen them for the role because
they are poor. It is an expression of God's freedom to choose.

**Int:** But how does this special role of the poor effect the
actual process of *doing* theology? The poor themselves are
hardly in a position to sit around writing books.

**Me:** As I see it liberation theology requires theologies to find
ways to place themselves so that they can respond to the poor.
This theology is not a particular dogmatic content. It is a
*method,* a way of *doing* theology, very well described by Alfred
T. Hennelly in his *Theologies in Conflict* (Orbis 1979). It is a
"percolate-up" rather than a trickle-down theology. It is
theology thought through from the perspective of the poor,
the powerless, the "underside of history," as Guttiérez calls it.
It addresses itself to a different agenda than do European and
U.S. academic theologies. It is not so preoccupied with
problems of belief and doubt—which bother only a relatively
small number of people and have become troublesome only

since the Enlightenment—but with the problems of justice and community.

**Int:** Do you plan to return to Latin America again soon?

**Me:** Yes, especially to the Carribean. The Carribean is a kind of bridge between the English and Spanish, the North and South, the Protestant and Catholic cultures of the two continents. I have visited Antigua, Cuba and Puerto Rico, but I want to get back soon. I do know one thing, however. My fantasies of *living* in Latin America have pretty well been shelved. I thought about it seriously a few years back. When I taught in Mexico City in 1979 I tried to imagine what it would be like to live there permanently. I love Mexico City, noise and smog and traffic and all. I think it is one of the most exciting cities in the world, but I knew after a few months that I could not really live there permanently. I feel welcome, but only as guest. I will always be in some measure a *gringo,* an outsider. I know my job is really one that has to be done in the U.S. I do not have the expatriate mentality.

**Int:** *Muchas gracias!*

**Me:** *De nada.*

# 11
# The Universal and the Local in Rome:
## A Memory, a Dream, an Interview

When Martin Luther first came to Rome in 1510 on some business connected with his religious order, the Augustinians, he is believed to have entered via the Piazza de Popolo which was then the "official" entrance to the Eternal City. According to the story, Luther fell to his knees under the gate which still stands there and cried out, "Hail Holy Rome, sanctified by the holy martyrs and by the blood shed there!" Later it seems, Luther became disgusted by the corruption, loose morals, and lax living of Rome. The visit rankled and eventually fed the motivation for his antipapal and antiroman zeal.

When I arrived in Rome in November, 1978, to spend part of my sabbatical leave studying, I came by way of the new international airport, was shortchanged by the taxi driver and could not have fallen on my knees anywhere without being run over by a motorbike. But nonetheless I still retain the memory of those golden days not only as some of the best I have ever lived but also as a time when I, like Luther, got a special kind of insight into things Roman. Mine, however, were different from his.

I lived in Rome at a residence on the historic old Piazza Navona called the Foyer Unitas. It is run by a group of animated Dutch Catholic nuns and as a kind of ecumenical gesture, they allow only non-Catholics and non-Italians to stay there. Consequently my breakfast companions were an English art historian, a German pastor, and two Swedish opera singers. It turned out to be one of the warmest and sunniest Novembers in recent Roman memory, and I spent the mornings plodding happily from cave to basilica to museum, and the afternoons in intense interviews with Vatican officials, leaders of the various political parties, journalists (who seem always willing to talk to anyone), scholars, waiters, street vendors, refugees from Brazil and Chile, Polish pilgrims, Danish tourists, and just about anyone else who would join me for a cup of expresso. All this went on during the first heady days of the pontificate of Pope John Paul II. He inevitably came up in every conversation and huge crowds gathered wherever he appeared. I remember one official of the Italian Socialist Party telling me that the pope was Rome's greatest natural resource, "a little like the Grand Canyon, our best source of foreign currencies." "Hail Rome, sanctified by the holy martyrs, etc.!"

Rome is indeed crass and worldly and seductive. Its spirituality is mixed with generous doses of gourmet provender and vintage wines. Corruption has not wholly disappeared from Rome since Luther's visit. But unlike Luther, whose shock deepened into revulsion, I found myself, to my own surprise, falling in love with Rome.

The following entries in my journal are typical expressions of the flushed euphoria I was feeling.

Nov. 4, 1978. Today I hiked from the Foyer to the Pantheon, then guidebook-in-hand ambled for three delicious hours through the streets and in and out of dank old churches. First to *San Luigi el Francese* which has three fabulous Caravaggio paintings based on the life of St. Matthew, all done toward the end of the 16th century. The book says that for years his paintings could not be publicly viewed because he depicted the saints and the Virgin realistically, with dirty feet. Then to *San Agostino,* built between 1479 and 1483 which was the favorite chapel of Christian humanists Castiglione, Sadoleto, Bembo, and Raphael all of whom erected little side chapels for their courtesans. Back to Piazza Navona (which now feels like home!) and the Church of *St. Agnes in Agony,* dedicated to a virgin saint who was martyred here after being stripped and humiliated at a brothel where she had been taken to get her to deny her faith. The story says that as her tormentors tore off her clothes God thoughtfully provided a miraculous growth of hair to cover her nakedness! She is buried at another St. Agnes on the opposite side of Rome. Will I ever have enough time in this fabulous city?

That night back at the Foyer Unitas, after a dinner at the Ristorante Panzironi of lasagna, eggplant parmesan and a demi of red, I fell asleep and sometime during the night I had a vivid dream.

I am having dinner in Rome with Marcello Mastroianni, the male lead in many of Federico Fellini's movies, and with Father Gerald O'Collins, a Catholic theologian teaching here in Rome who had invited me to lunch at the Gregorian University a few days before. We are all laughing uncontrollably because we have just noticed that Mastroianni and I are wearing nearly identical ties, shirts and sports jackets. Then, wiping my eyes, I rise, raise my glass and tell them I have decided to be baptized in the Tiber. They approve.

Only weeks later did I begin to discern the meaning of the dream. Baptized in the Tiber! Even in the cultural and culinary capital of Christendom, and even when I am beginning to look like one of "them," somewhere way down in my unconscious recesses I am still the Baptist kid.

The dream turned out to be at least partially prophetic. It was while living in the Piazza Navona, next door to the church of San Agnace, hearing the splashing of Bernini's Fountain of the Four Rivers, engulfed by centuries of Catholic history and the vastness of the universal church, that I rediscovered the local congregation.

It happened on my second Sunday morning in Rome. I

attended the popular grass-roots Christian community called Saint Paul's that had been founded nine years before by the Benedictine Abbot Giovanni Franzoni. At the time of my visit the community was meeting about halfway between the Pyramid of Cestius and the Basilica of St. Paul's Outside the Walls in a gaunt abandoned warehouse in a nondescript section of Rome on the Via Ostiense No. 152b.

St. Paul's congregation is a mixed group including professionals and intellectuals but also a scattering of working class folks. The liturgy was open and informal. Father Franzoni, a big, bearlike man, did not really "lead" it. He wandered around the altar and the pulpit as lay men and women took most of the responsibility. Instead of a single homily, five people gave short statements on the text of the day. The whole congregation recited the eucharistic prayer together and at the Communion the people walked respectfully to the altar table and helped themselves to the consecrated bread and wine. There was spirited singing, lots of announcements, a good deal of talk about politics, a collection, a warm "kiss of peace," and an atmosphere that clearly said the members liked to be there and were in no hurry whatever to go home.

The spoken parts of the service were translated for me in part by Ed Grace, an American who has lived for years in Rome and who has become one of the world's best-informed writers and interpreters of Christian grass-roots communities. From him I learned that these base communities in which lay people play a much more central role than they ever have in Catholic parishes, are spreading quickly all over Italy. There are already hundreds of them and shortly after I left they held a huge national gathering in Rome. I later learned they represent a worldwide wave. There are over forty thousand such communities in Brazil, and other Latin American countries are not far behind. In fact the rapid rise of these Christian-base communities may constitute the most important change occurring in the Catholic Church today. As lay-controlled and politically involved local congregations they could have a profound effect on the future of that church and

on all of Christianity. They could even move the world
Christian church away from its hierarchial, clerically domin-
ated form, and transform it eventually into a truly participatory organism, although I doubt this will happen very soon,
especially with John Paul II at the helm of Peter's bark.

Later in the week, a few days after I had visited St. Paul, met
Father Franzoni and eaten a three-hour-long Sunday dinner
with some of the members, Ed Grace asked me if he could
interview me for a weekly ecumenical publication called *Com
Nuovi Tempi* which he writes for. I agreed, and as the interview
proceeded and with St. Paul's on my mind I found myself
talking with affection about my own local church (Old
Cambridge Baptist Church), the "base community" of which I
am a part, and its importance in my faith journey. "NTC"
stands (I think) for "*Nuovo Tempi* correspondent."

**NTC:** You are a well-known Baptist theologian who teaches
at Harvard University and whose books about religion in
contemporary society have been translated into numerous
languges (from *Secular City* through *Turning East*). But little is
known about you as a man of faith who lives his eucharistic life
within a believing community. Could you tell us something
about the community you are in. When it began? How it
evolved?

**COX:** The local church community I belong to is about one
hundred fifty years old; it began as a Baptist congregation, the
first one in the area of the University. About fifteen years ago a
development began in it which has become quite extraordinary. The pastor and some of the leaders of the congregation
began taking the idea of the ministry of the laity so seriously
that the laity began sharing in the preparation and leading of
the worship services, in pastoral calling, in planning and
executing the Christian education and in carrying out the
social mission of the church.

This developed to such an extent that when the pastor left
eight years ago the congregation was faced with the decision of
whether they should call another minister—as it is done in local

Baptist congregations—whom they would have to educate into this lay-controlled church, or whether they would continue at least for a year or two without such outside help being called, and instead simply share the ministry more widely in the congregation. Finally they took up this second idea. This meant some fundamental changes: for example we no longer hold that a person must be ordained to lead us in the blessing and distribution of the Communion elements.

We do have deacons in the church who prepare and train people in the other leadership functions of the church. But these deacons are elected and rotate every two or three years.

Also everything that needs to be done now includes both men and women equally; this means that any Sunday both men and women will be leading the service, presiding over Communion, preaching, and whatever.

Likewise, we have become more engaged in social and political action around our own area and nationally.

**NTC:** Was there any relationship between the church's development of its laity and its concern for social-political problems?

**COX:** Yes, there was a direct relationship. The more the lay people assumed a leadership role in the gathered phases of the community, that is around the worship and the hearing and studying of the Word, the more the actual *concerns* of lay people were brought into the formation of the liturgy.

In those days people were terribly upset about the war in Vietnam. So this naturally came into the liturgy, creating in turn an outward movement of the community and its individual members into various efforts in political life.

In the last years because many of our members either work in the health care field or else have experienced family sickness, we became aware that the present hospital setup in the U.S. serves mainly the wealthy and middle class, creating an enormous injustice for the rest of the population; so we have gotten interested in the problem of health care distribution.

**NTC:** Could you describe a typical Sunday liturgy for us?

**COX:** One of the most important things about our community is that we open the liturgy every Sunday to what we call "concerns" and "celebrations"; this might be parallel to "bidding prayers" in the Anglican tradition or "testimonies" as we used to call them in the Baptist tradition. Anyone at all, including people who just walk in off the streets, can get up at a certain point and say to the whole congregation what is important to them or what is troubling them or what they are happy about or what they want to give thanks for or ask help for at this moment.

Virtually everything can happen: someone is looking for an apartment; someone is terribly sad or has lost a friend; someone needs prayers for a sick person; someone is angry. This brings the life of the real world, the nasty and wonderful little things which life is really made up of, right into the center of worship. These things are all gathered together in a pastoral prayer before we share the eucharist.

Another thing that might be of interest is that we found that the more the laity prepared and became involved presiding over our worship, the more the actual breaking of bread and sharing of the wine has become central to our worship.

I can't quite explain why this is.

It used to be the tradition in Baptist churches to have Communion about once a month or so; it was not emphasized. But we have made the eucharist much more central. I should also say our community has become less "denominational." I think it is the experience of many grass-root communities. Once you have begun to open up like this, people from various traditions and backgrounds begin to come in, including a number of persons in our congregation who are not Baptists and who really don't want to become Baptists.

This has meant, for example, that we must reexamine our traditional notion of baptism only for adults. We now have a pluralistic view of the possibilities of baptism. This has not made us popular among other Baptist congregations.

**NTC:** How has this affected you as a theologian? In short, is being a member of this congregation essential to you as a theologian?

**COX:** I would say in all candor that this congregation is not only important but is absolutely integral to my own life as a human being, and therefore, my life as a theologian, as a teacher of theology and as a researcher in this field. I know that this is true, but I sometimes have difficulty explaining how it is true.

Let me give just one example. In the last chapter of my most recent book which is called *Turning East,* I have a description of the importance of community in the appeal of the new Eastern religions. One of the reasons why people seem to join them in the U.S.A. is that they find a sense of community in them. I am concerned how this sense of belonging to each other, and "sharing each other's burdens," as the Bible says, has often evaporated in many Christian churches. We have a hierarchical or even a kind of public institutional view of the churches. The church is *there,* and you go for a special service which the church provides for you; but it is not really a community.

Moreover, I have been persuaded that, especially in our modern industrial society, we are deprived of the opportunity for friendship and sharing, for a relationship with people which is not competitive. We are deprived of this especially by the capitalistic mode of organizing the world which is to set people against one another. It is built on the engine of competition and it needs to expand markets and, therefore, to instill the need for accumulating things, buying things.

When you are living under that kind of distorted picture of life, all that many people have left is the nuclear family: the mother, the father, and the children. And this is not enough. It puts entirely too much strain on that diminished family which sometimes causes it to crack.

So I think that a small but intense Christian community can be a kind of modern surrogate for the old extended family that we used to live in. This is the secret under all the description I have given of my church community: people really do care for one another, do share one another's difficult moments, and there is even one group in the congregation of twelve families that decided (eight years ago) to buy an old apartment house and to live in it cooperatively.

This has all influenced me in ways which are all hard to describe, but important.

**NTC:** Has this center of twelve families of the community become an island unto itself, sharing its own burdens but not those of the outside world?

**COX:** I would say quite honestly that the first couple of years the community fell into that pattern somewhat. There was such a need for adjustment in living this close together that there was a certain tendency to draw a circle around and to have less to do with the outside. I don't think this is the situation any longer. This "community within the community" now provides leadership in the larger Christian community, within political movements, on the housing commission, in the PTA, and in the women's movement. So I don't think that this core community is just a place of withdrawal. It has provided a "home base" so we can sally forth into the world.

**NTC:** The following is a question rarely asked to theologians, but how do you respond at that central point of where the Word of God confronts *you?* What does all this mean to you as a man of prayer?

**COX:** I would have to answer that in the context of "hearing" and "responding to" the Word *in a community of people.* I am not satisfied with those metaphors of "hearing" and "responding to" the Word which seem individualistic: the proclamation which some*one* hears and then something happens.

For me the response is almost always a response in which I share what the Word says to me and what I think it requires of me with people who are close to me and who share my life.

The Word of God shared in the community has meant to me, especially since I have been involved in the community in these last years, a provisional liberation from the pressures of society, from the demand for constant competition and from the need for aggrandizement. I put less value on "career" for example.

I don't think that one person or one family can successfully resist the poisoning effects of an accumulating—competitive society (I mean soul poisoning) without the support of other people who are sharing that same kind of alternative life.

**NTC:** Anything else?

**COX:** Yes, one thing that we have learned about in our community is that simplicity and a certain type of lighthearted asceticism are not only possible but help us to discover the underlying joy of being Christian, being in the realm of Grace. And I don't believe the realm of Grace is something that has to begin in some other world. I think you can have a foretaste of it and that it makes itself real in the community of faith.

So for me *liberation* is the word that describes this best. It includes an ongoing personal liberation that enables me to see that the activity of God in our world today is best caught with terms such as "release from bondage," "new hope," and "new possibilities."

This is why theologies of liberation are so characteristic of our times. But you have to be undergoing personal "liberations" from what it is that is keeping you from being all that God intends you to be in order to understand what people who are more drastically oppressed hear in the Word of God.

**NTC:** You had the opportunity to participate in an Italian grass-roots community, the community of Saint Paul in Rome which was founded by the Benedictine Abbot Giovanni Franzoni and his lay community some nine years ago. What was your impression there?

**COX:** I would say—although I have only been in Italy for ten days—I felt happy and touched, and very much at home even though I couldn't understand much of what was being said at Saint Paul's. It reminded me of my home church community, the one I've just described. Even the kind of not-completely efficient or smooth-running organization of the worship, the allowance for a little bit of slippage here and there, the participation of the women and the voicing of concerns.

When the woman stood up and spoke about her anguish over the death of someone in her school, I immediately thought of the kind of things that happen in our church community.

And I also have the suspicion that when we look around the world today the important thing going on in the Christian church may not be the exciting new theological movement, it may be this spectacular growth of authentic, Christian communities at the grass roots level. And I think that goes across the boundaries of denominations and nations. It is going on just everywhere. A new, and I think a more genuine form of Christian congregational life is emerging.

I think it is the working of the Spirit.

The Spirit is reforming the church in ways that a lot of people don't even notice, because this reformation is not being carried out by some great magisterial reformers sitting in Geneva or somewhere. It is being done by the people, which is how it has to be done.

(Here the interview, which appeared only in CNT ends. It is, incidentally, a *real* interview, not like the one in the previous chapter.)

As I sit here and reread my journal notes and the interview from three years ago in Rome, I am even more convinced that my dream of baptism in the Tiber had a sibylline quality to it. One friend of mine used to say that the Christian church of the future should be a mixture of Eastern Orthodox and Quaker. He meant it should include the Byzantine brocade and pageantry but should also cultivate the personal commitment to peace and justice and the nondogmatic openness of the Friends.

Could the same thing be accomplished by a mixture of San Agostino and grass-roots communities; of fabulous legends à la St. Agnes and real local participation; of baroque excess and spare simplicity: of Roman and Baptist? Why cannot the saints have both halos and dirty feet? My fondest fantasies about the church of the future run along these lines. Is it all visionary?

On my last night at the *Foyer Unitas* I could not sleep. I got up, dressed, and looked out the window onto the Piazza Navona. It was empty, and a soft rain was falling on the paving stones. I wandered into the little library of the Foyer with its neat shelves of books in several languages, thoughtfully kept there by the nuns for their international guests. Among the English language volumes I noticed a copy of Nathaniel Hawthorne's *The Marble Faun* first published in 1860, the literary record of an earlier New Englander's infatuation with Rome. Just the day before I had seen the original statue of the faun at the Capitoline Palace: a half-human, half-animal creature clothed only in a fur sash across its chest, with curly hair and pointed ears. I had promised myself I would look up the novel when I got back home but here it was; so I reached up and took it down, sank into a chair and began to page through it.

It seems that what fascinated Hawthorne about the faun was its being a creature that, as half-human and half-animal, mediated between separate worlds, "sympathizing with each, comprehending the speech of either race and interpreting the whole existence of one to the other." I could see why Hawthorne, fresh from Salem and the gray ghosts of his Puritan forebears had fallen for Rome, and why the marble faun had become the Siren-center of his allurement. Rome is the layered depository of millennia of Western culture—pagan, romanesque, baroque, and all the rest. It positively exudes the sweet aroma of everything the Puritans detested, repressed and probably secretly hankered for.

My mind was getting groggy. I tried to imagine what the first settlers of Cambridge, Mass., would have thought of Caravaggio's fleshy and erotic "Amor Victorious Over Worldly Might, Art and Science" which he was painting at about the time they were cutting down the chestnut forests and founding Harvard College. It seemed to me in the solitude of the little library at 3:00 A.M. that those two worlds, of Cotton Mather and Castiglione, so close in time, so removed in temperament, were almost as disparate as the two fused in the marvelous marble faun. Hawthorne needed a symbol of how the two could be brought in touch because they were two sides of his own soul. The marble faun supplied it.

After only a few minutes, my eyes felt heavy. I closed them and my mind began to wander again. I saw Giovanni Franzoni, the hulking Benedictine in an open-collared shirt, with his ears ever so slightly pointed and a fur sash across his chest. Was the Saint Paul base community on Via Ostiense a link between Caravaggio, Bernini, and San Luigi del Francesi on the one hand and Old Cambridge Baptist Church on the other?

A church bell rang. It was 3:30 A.M. I stood to put the book back on the shelf but opened it one more time. A previous reader, possibly an earlier guest at the Foyer, had underlined a passage: "Side by side with the massiveness of the Roman past, all matters that we handle or dream of nowadays look evanescent and visionary alike." Now I closed the book firmly and replaced it. I was ready to leave Rome, with its "massive past," and return home. But I knew that Vincenzo and Teri and the people from the warehouse on the Via Ostiense were not just visionaries, and what they were "handling" was not just evanescent. The future church they and I both hope for is already coming to birth. It is truly universal and also radically local. Both St. Agnes with her long hair flowing and Mary Dyer, the Quaker who was hanged on Boston Common find their places in it. It is catholic and congregational, global and grass roots. It has room for Caravaggio and Castiglione, and the Puritans. It is a delicate creature yet, to be sure, and fragile, but we are living at the moment of its birth and we may live to see its flowering.

Hail Holy Rome, sanctified by the holy martyrs and by the blood shed here! Blessed by the furry sidelocks of the marble faun and the smell of baked lasagna; trampled by tourists and drowned out by Fiat engines; enlivened by sunburned opera singers, cosmopolitan nuns, jeweled courtesan chapels and a Polish pope; harboring a grass-roots community where people still get the message, despite (or because of) it all! Sorry, Luther. Hail Holy Rome! How could anyone *not* fall in love with you?

# 12
# Fear and Trembling in Tehran

On January 4, 1979, the following account, written by me, appeared on the first page of the Boston *Herald American*. Since it was written in the breathless aftermath of the incident itself I am reproducing it here just as I first wrote it.

It began blandly enough as my flight from Tel Aviv touched down shortly after sunrise for what was supposed to be a mere change of planes. As I glanced out the window of the El Al jet at the snowcapped peaks that frame the capital of Iran, the only thing that seemed even vaguely ominous were the droves of troop carriers and soldiers at the airport. But that did not surprise me. I knew the Shah had just instituted a military government. Besides, I had only an hour and a half layover until my Air Afghan flight would waft me to Kabul, Afghanistan, the next stop on my sabbatical journey.

Inside the terminal, I immediately began to feel uneasy. No flight announcement boards were operating. Crowds of people stood around in clusters or sat on piles of baggage in the departure lounge, waiting (I soon learned) to get on any outgoing flight. Occasionally an announcement crackled over the loudspeaker in Persian, French, or incomprehensible English. The dingy waiting area was decorated only with pictures of the Shah and his family and with dusty black and white photos of ancient Persian ruins. Soldiers armed with automatic rifles, their eyes nervously darting in all directions, were everywhere. I pitied the anxious-looking refugees. I was glad I was a transit passenger with a confirmed ticket clutched in my palm.

"Sorry, sir, Air Afghan stopped flying out of here last week," a prim Iranian Airlines employee finally told me, after I had waited a half hour in line to ask directions. "I doubt very much if they will be flying out of here again in the near future," she added.

"Well," I answered, smiling widely, "I guess I'll just have to get on some other flight out then." I searched her face for some sign of encouragement.

"I'm afraid so," she said, avoiding my eyes and pointing the way to the jammed outer departure lounge, "Good luck." I tried to ask her another question, but she had already turned to the next customer. She had nothing more to offer me now. In a single sentence, I had been transformed from a nervous but smug "transit" passenger into just one more faceless refugee trying to get out of Iran.

The outer departure area was not a cheerful sight. The airport restaurant was closed and only tepid tea and last week's dried-up biscuits were being sold at a snack bar. Whenever a flight seemed ready to leave, crowds of would-be passengers mobbed the ticketing desk, shouting and shoving. Clutching my useless ticket, jostled by desperate refugees, stuck in a country undergoing a revolution, I finally staked out a tiny piece of floor where I could put down my suitcase and collect my thoughts.

A few hours passed. I noticed, encamped near me, a young West German engineer who told me he had been waiting there for four days trying to get out. He asked me if I had a visa for Iran and I said, "Of course not, I'm only in transit." But with no visa, on top of my unusable flight ticket, he gently pointed out I not only could not fly out, I also could not leave the airport terminal. Armed gurds at the door allowed only people with valid visas to leave the building in order to sleep or eat in Tehran.

"Where can I get a visa?" I asked.

"You can't," he answered. "They used to issue them at the airport, but they don't anymore. No one is ever in that office."

It took several minutes for the full import of his remark to register. When it did, it occurred to me that there was only one thing left to do: Call the American Embassy, explain my plight, and ask for help. Since there were no phone books at the one coin telephone in the lounge, I looked for an American in the crowd and found a husky Ohioan, a departing former employee of an American electronics firm, who told me he had a seat on a Japan Airlines flight. I asked him if he happened to know the number of the American Embassy. He said no, he didn't, and besides, the telephones were not working. As he was talking, his flight was called. He also wished me "good luck" in doubtful tones, and strode through the barrier to his plane. I waved to him limply.

By mid-evening even the snack bar had closed and I was starving. The terminal seemed quieter except for the buzzing flourescent lights overhead. The curfew prevented new people from arriving at the airport, and Iranians and foreigners with visas had returned to the city. Now I was virtually alone in the lounge, sharing it with a few airport employees, some yawning soldiers, and a bored woman at the Duty Free counter. Nodding, but unwilling to fall asleep lest I miss a possible flight, I began to experience a sense of unreality, enhanced no doubt by fatigue and hunger. Just then a young man in an official airport uniform walked over to me, introduced himself cordially in good English, and asked if he could help. I felt like kissing his hand, but I simply told him my plight. He nodded, said he thought he could help and asked if I was hungry. I allowed that I was. Smiling, he led me to the Duty Free counter.

This move puzzled me since I had noticed that the Duty Free

shop sold only liquor, cigarettes, and perfume. But I thought he might be making some special arrangement for me. He was. But not for me. Speaking to the attendant in Persian, he handed me some Iranian money to give her. I did. She then asked me the normal questions one answers at a Duty Free shop: name, passport number, flight number. I gave her the first two, but told her I had no flight number. She wrote something on her receipt machine, cranked the lever and handed me a copy. Then she handed my new found friend four bottles of J. & B. Scotch. He turned and walked past the guards, out of the airport and into the night. I never saw him again. But I had just unwittingly helped him buy what someone later told me was about $200 worth of booze for the black market.

Now I was not only hungry and tired, but angry—at my supposed friend and at myself for allowing someone to bilk me into using my passport number to buy whiskey. But now, at least, I knew what I had to do. I had to get out. I was ready to cheat, lie, shove, bribe. I wanted to get on any plane going anywhere. But the worst was still to come.

At about 8 A.M., just after an Air India flight had left, stranding dozens of would-be passengers who had found some way to get to the airport despite the curfew, an armed policeman came up to me and ordered me to follow him. At first I was puzzled but when he marched me to the Duty Free counter and the attendant nodded when he pointed to me, I suspected I knew what it was about. I had technically bought whiskey at the Duty Free and sold it to an Iranian citizen. I was a black marketeer in alcohol—in a Muslim country. I wondered idly how many other hapless foreigners had been similarly duped. The policeman, who spoke only Persian, talked to me through the Duty Free attendant. I was right. They had my passport number. I had bought four bottles of Scotch. I did not have them. Now the policeman spoke emphatically and the attendant translated quickly, as though she had made the speech before: If I knew what was good for me, I would now buy whiskey for this policeman.

The policeman stared at me, his thumb near the stock of his gun. The attendant watched me coolly. I had read something about Iranian prisons. I also knew a little about the rigidity, however hypocritically enforced, of the Muslim rules about liquor. But I also knew that blackmail is a bottomless pit. So I did the only thing I could. I turned and walked away. The policeman did not follow.

For some odd reason I now felt quite calm for the first time in many hours. I knew that objectively speaking my situation was worse than ever. I had seen police at the flight exit gate comparing the Duty Free receipts with the packages the passengers were carrying. I realized that even if I did get onto a flight, I would still have to get past that barrier. I sat for a full half-hour and then decided that even though I had been tricked by an airport official, I should not now lose all my confidence in human nature. I needed help, and I was ready to ask for it again. I waited.

At about 2:30 A.M., a middle-aged Iranian woman turned on a small light behind the Air France counter. At the same moment people began appearing at the entrance gate for what turned out to be a flight to Delhi. I raced to the counter, put my mouth close to the woman's ear, and hoarsely whispered my whole story—the sting, the blackmail, all of it. I knew it was risky. She might be part of the conspiracy. She could easily signal the sentry at just that moment, and I would find myself in jail. Raptly examining the papers in front of her, she only looked up once as I talked. When I finished, she told me I'd simply have to wait with all the other standby passengers—and there were very many.

I waited. The flight came in. The ticketed passengers boarded. The stand-bys pressed around the desk. The lady announced to the crowd that there were only four stand-by places available and began to read the list. My name was first. She handed me a boarding pass and only allowed her eyes to meet mine for one second.

One more hurdle to cross: the flight exit gate where police were comparing receipts from the Duty Free with the packages people were carrying. The line moved sowly. I arrived at the desk. The officer checked my passport number against the list of passengers on this flight who had bought things. I held my breath. My name was not on it. Since I had not had a flight when I purchased the whiskey, the slip had not yet come to this desk. I walked out into the dawn, boarded the Air France flight and in twenty minutes I was on the way to Delhi.

Over exquisite expresso, croissants, butter, and marmalade, I thanked God for that occasional inefficiency of a bureaucracy that allows a receipt not to show up. For Air France, the jet engine, and the feel of wheels leaving a runway. But especially for one middle-aged woman I'll never see again. To me, she represents the very best of the long-suffering, courageous Persian people, and she deserves, as they do, to live in a freer, less corrupt, less brutalized Iran than the one they live in today.

My account ends there, and reading it two years later still makes me tremble. But in retrospect I am sure that terrifying interruption in a sabbatical journey nonetheless marked a long step in my faith journey.

When the Air France jet landed in New Delhi a few hours later it was still morning. The scene at the airport was hectic. No one seemed to be in charge. Some arriving passengers staggered under piles of luggage. Others stood empty-handed and seemed bewildered. People who looked vaguely official shouted mysterious commands. There were no real lines in front of the customs and immigration gates, only crowded clumps of people jostling and shoving.

Still, I did not mind a bit. I was in no hurry. I was out of Tehran and I thought it was nice to be some place where people were trying to get *into* a country instead of trying to leave it. I calmly surveyed the seething pandemonium around me, waited until the crowd abated slightly, then breezed past the formidable line of uniformed officials without so much as opening a suitcase.

Outside the main airport building the sun was just beginning to rise. Traffic was still sparse. I took a cab to the Vikram Hotel, ate another (this time, English) breakfast and checked into my room.

There in the room, all of a sudden, it hit me. All the terror and tears I had artfully held at bay in Tehran erupted. I began to wail and sob. I fell onto the bed and shook. My nose began to bleed. I realized that throughout those horrid hours in Tehran I had been in a state of shock, flying on automatic pilot. Instinctively realizing that to collapse and cry there would only have worsened the situation, my body and my psyche had colluded to keep me cool and functioning, at least externally. The stopper had stayed in place until I was safely in my room in New Delhi, but now like some long dormant Mt. St. Helen's, it all blew.

After what seemed like an hour of chest-heaving and groaning I eventually calmed down, washed my face and sat myself in a chair facing a window overlooking a courtyard filled with earthen jars and piles of lumber, to add up what had happened. One of the first things that occurred to me was that I had been willing to do just about anything to get out of Tehran. Where were my moral principles, my respect for ethical absolutes? I am not sure exactly what lengths I would have gone to in order to get out. Cheat or lie? Surely. Physically harm or restrain someone else (despite all my nonviolent rhetoric and belief)? Probably. Kill someone? Probably not, but how would I have felt after a week, two weeks, a month, several months? Those hours in Tehran gave me a sense of respect for people *in extremis* who violate this or that accepted ethical sanction in what to them appear to be extraordinary circumstances. It did not convert me into a "situational" ethicist, whatever that may be. It did make me a little more aware of the kind of behavior of which I myself might be capable when pressed to it.

An ironical parenthesis: as I stewed and fumed in the Tehran airport, one idea that appears in my original account and that constantly kept entering my mind was, "If only I could get to the American Embassy then I'd be okay." It is a thought that often occurs to American citizens when they get into trouble on foreign soil. Or at least it used to. I was enraged that I could not phone the embassy (because of the telephone operator's strike) or get there by taxi (because I had no visa and could not leave the main airport building). Despite my frequent criticisms of U.S. foreign policy and my support of those who were trying even then to get rid of the Shah, I pictured myself at times safe and sound in the embassy, looked after by the staff, protected by the Marines, eventually evacuated from Iran under the powerful auspices of the U.S. government. Later, when the American embassy was occupied and the hostages taken, I realized just how naïve I had been.

Another thought that occurred to me as I sat on my cot in the Vikram that morning, stanching my nosebleed with paper towels, was that for whatever reason, I had not prayed to God to get me out of Tehran. I had schemed and fretted. I had tried to meditate a couple times, mainly to get my mind away from being obsessed with the armed militia and the locked gates and the crowds of would-be refugees. But the first time I prayed was when I felt the wheels of the Air France jet leave the runway and I knew at last I was out. It was not a prayer of supplication but of gratitude: "Thank you God for getting me the hell out of there."

Schleiermacher versus Bonhoeffer? The former had claimed in the early nineteenth century that religion springs from our absolute dependence on God. Although I am sure Schleiermacher himself was not referring to some kind of supine spinelessness, still he represents for me the kind of spiritual dependence I was raised on, the "let me to thy bosom fly" piety of the Baptist hymnal. In any case, he might have been more sympathetic to the idea that being trapped in the Tehran airport in the midst of a revolution and harassed by armed militiamen teaches one something about powerlessness and our need to turn to Something higher and more powerful than ourselves, not as an admission of cowardice but as a recognition of reality.

Bonhoeffer, on the other hand, writing in the twentieth century came to believe that we should not settle for a God we call on only in our moments of weakness and need. He had a sense of that weakness and suffering of God which calls forth human strength and fortitude. Bonhoeffer did not come to this position easily. His years in prison under the Nazis taught him a certain kind of powerlessness. Still, he believed we should not think of God as a *deus ex machina*, a "magic helper" who stoops to our weakness, but as a full participant in the suffering and the struggle all human beings undergo.

Although without even thinking about it, I followed more a Bonhoeffer than what I have called a Schleiermacher course here, I am not sure that this description is fair to either of them or gives an accurate picture of how my faith functions. Before and after the Tehran airport incident I have found myself praying, sometimes almost unconsciously, "Get me out of here!" or "Please make it stop hurting!" or "Keep her safe, God. I can't do anything."

I do not believe such primal prayers can be ruled out of the life of faith. We will pray, or think, or at least feel such supplications as long as we live and continue to stumble up against the outer limits of all human powers. But Bonhoeffer was surely right that God does not will us to be what psychotherapists call "passive dependent" personalities. One such therapist, M. Scott Peck puts it this way in his excellent book *The Road Less Traveled* (Simon & Schuster, 1980). Dependency, he says, is "the inability to experience wholeness or to function adequately without the certainty that one is being actively cared for by another" (p. 98). Peck goes on to explain that this kind of pathological dependency is not the same thing at all as what are often referred to as "dependency needs or feelings" which are quite normal.

I think this is the key to the distinction between the type of theology I have identified with Schleiermacher. "No matter how strong we are," Peck writes, "no matter how caring and responsible and adult," we all need to be taken care of now and then. No matter how mature and grownup, we would all like to have a caring parent figure around. For most of us, however, "these desires and feelings do not rule our lives; they are not the predominant theme of our existence." When they cease to be just one aspect among others of our psychic structure and begin to predominate, begin to be the feature that motivates us most of the time, then we have ceased having normal "dependency needs" and have become what psychotherapists call "passive dependent" personalities. Thinking about what prayer had and had not meant for me during and after the time in Tehran taught me more than any number of books could.

The Tehran airport! Will I ever forget it? Hardly. It imposed on me an unwelcome interruption in my sabbatical journey, but at the same time it moved me a long way in my faith journey. I still cannot honestly say I am thankful it happened. I can say I am glad I got out and that I hope if God has anything else to teach me about my personal ethical frailty or my style of prayer, the lesson can be communicated in a less nerve-racking environment. Still, I know only too well that we do not choose the times or the places where that kind of growth takes place. That's the odd thing about faith journeys. We may be moving fastest just when we think we are most immobilized.

# 13
# Past and Future in Hiroshima

During the summer of 1978 I flew to Kyoto, the ancient capital of Japan to attend an international, interreligious conference on peace. The gathering included Christians, Jews, Hindus, Buddhists, Shintoists, and Muslims. At the end of that conference, a group of the Japanese hosts invited me to accompany them on a visit to Hiroshima. I accepted, but reluctantly. I knew it would not be easy.

We sped southward to Hiroshima on the famous bullet train. Arriving in a few hours, we were welcomed by the Hiroshima maidens in their flowered kimonas, given bouquets and taken almost immediately to the simple plaque which marks the spot where on August 6, 1945, the first atomic bomb was exploded. We stood there quietly. I thought for a moment of my ancestor Joseph Cox and the mass grave of the Paoli Massacre victims. From bayonets to atom bombs. From 150 to 90,000. Then our host said it was time to move on. The others moved but for some reason my legs would not respond to the signals of my mind. I seemed to be paralyzed, at least for the moment, riveted in place. It was two or three minutes before I could turn and join my compatriots on the bus. I was a little embarrassed, but later I recognized what had happened.

For years I had known that something history-changing had occurred on August 6, 1945. But I had known it with my mind. Now as I stood there, the message seemed to soak into my body tissue and the marrow of my bones. I *knew* in a wholly different way that on this spot *everything changed.* "Everything changed," as Einstein has said, "except the way we think." We still *think* about balances of power, defensive systems, national security, in a world in which all of those things have become irrelevant because our species could go the way of the pterodactyl. But, unlike those creatures, the disappearance of our species could drag along with it the entire ecosystem or at least our fragile planet's capacity to bear most forms of life with, I am told, the possible exception of the cockroach. All this I now *knew* at Hiroshima as I had never known it before. "This," the little plaque and the bouquets and the place itself said to me, "is *it.*"

We are the first generation in history to face this. No wonder it is taking us a while to recognize it. There have been fifty-seven generations, by my count, since the first people followed Jesus; perhaps a hundred since Moses; two hundred or more since Abraham. All of those generations have had to face challenges: hunger, war, pestilence, disease, tragedy. But no generation until ours has had to contemplate what we must: that our species now has within its power the capacity to destroy itself and most other forms of life. No wonder we don't like to think about this often. Still what paralyzed me at Hiroshima was the thought that *now* is the time and perhaps there will be no later time.

In Tom Stoppard's puzzling play, *Rosencrantz and Guildenstern Are Dead,* based on Shakespeare's *Hamlet,* the two main figures who spied on Hamlet for the king converse with each other in the last act. The forces that have been set in motion up to that point cannot be called back. Everyone else is dead: Hamlet, the queen, the king. It is the final scene. Rosencrantz and Guildenstern are in a boat heading across the English

Channel. They think they are safe. Actually, the letter of "safe conduct" they are carrying directs that the bearers should be put to death. These two are not really evil men. Their acts seem quite minor compared with the consequences which resulted from the events they set in motion. Finally, Rosencrantz turns to Guildenstern and says rather pathetically, "There must have been a time somewhere near the beginning when we could have said 'No.' "

What my frozen limbs were saying to me in Hiroshima was that this is the time for me and for all Christians and all human beings to say no. We must say no now so as not to find ourselves five or ten years from now having to look back to where we crossed a point of no return and ask ourselves why we did not say no.

When I got home from Japan I had a hard time describing what had happened to me in Hiroshima. I found that most people still think of the peacemaking task of the churches and synagogues as something the bishops, the Berrigans, the theologians, the rabbis, the preachers do. Most church people also consider peacemaking something like an elective course, something you take if you have time after your required courses are fulfilled. Worst of all, we have been for peace in general, abstractly conceived. There has been a lack of specificity, no concreteness in our witness for peace.

After my visit in Hiroshima I knew—I *knew*—that now all this must go. We have to stop having an elitist understanding of peacemaking, as something done by experts. We have to stop thinking of it as an optional activity. We have to make it something as specific as it can possibily be.

A few weeks after I returned from Japan I saw a poll conducted in California in which a random sample of people were asked two questions: Do you believe that there will be a nuclear war, and do you believe you will survive it? Eighty-four percent of those responding said that yes, they believed there would be a nuclear war and no, they did not believe they would personally survive it.

I was shocked and skeptical about that poll, but it bothered me so much, that a few days later, I tried it on one of my classes at Harvard. I picked a class which was as representative as possible, with Harvard undergraduates, divinity students, and students from other divisions of the university, about a hundred in all. To my shock and chagrin, roughly the same percentage responded the same way. About 80 to 85 percent said yes, they believed there would be a nuclear war and no, they did not believe they would personally survive it. Counting the hands and writing down the numbers on my classroom blackboard I saw something I had not seen before. Nuclear war is not just a political or even a moral question. It is a theological and religious challenge of the first order.

The problem is fatalism: "it's going to happen." We are witnessing a return to a Karmic mentality, to seeing ourselves as helpless victims in the hands of some implacable Kismet. The heart of biblical faith—that human beings are created free and responsible, and mandated to be the stewards and nurturers of the earth and of one another—all this is called into question if we believe some awful fate awaits us and there is not one damn thing we can do about it. Perhaps a bit provincially, I was skeptical of a California poll, seeing California people as a bit crazy and apocalyptic anyway: the San Andreas fault mentality. However, my skepticism had to be set aside when my own students responded the same way. These are not people who are living today as though there will be no tomorrow. We like to think of Harvard as one of the last bastions of "delayed gratification," as a place where people work now with the thought that at some future moment they will be able to give leadership in the various sectors of society. There were students in my class from the medical school, the education school, the law school, divinity school. They were staying up late at night working on projects and term papers, and yet, in some dark region of their hearts, eighty-five out of a hundred did not believe they had a future to prepare for.

I have come to believe that this is a *spiritual* contradiction. The kind of healing and redemption the gospel promises can't simply come through words to people who are confronting that kind of non-future. We need the experience of unlocking the contradiction. Here is where churches and synagogues can contribute something that no one else can contribute. We can remove the taboo on the outrage, the screaming and crying which must be in the hearts of people who see no future for themselves. Remove the social taboo and let people cry out! As the children of Israel cried out in their misery and imprisonment, in their servitude in Egypt—"and God heard them." But God heard them only when they cried out, not before; not when their anger and their outrage were locked in silence. When they called out, God heard, not before.

A year after my transforming visit to Hiroshima I spent some days in Utah helping people who were organizing against the MX missile system. Again the spectre of Karmic fatalism, the numbing mood of resignation. At that time the MX was to be a kind of trolley system with 4,600 stops in which, through some sleight of hand, two hundred intercontinental missiles were to be hidden, and moved from one to another, in a grotesque caricature of the old carnival shell game. I met no one in Utah who wanted the MX put there. No one wanted to live in the area designated as the "great sponge" (the place to absorb some enemy's massive first strike against all of these sites in order to find those two hundred missiles). No one wanted it, but everyone felt helpless, powerless, resigned, enraged, believing they could do nothing. So I have come to the conviction that our greatest enemy now is *not* the Russians, or the Chinese, or the Iranians, or the Pentagon—our greatest enemy is our own fatalism. This Karmic resignation is tied, I believe, to our incapacity to cry out.

The inheritors of biblical faith have yet another conviction in addition to our belief in human responsibility. It is that in the life and ministry, the death and resurrection of Jesus of Nazareth, God has taken upon Godself the flesh of our human species. We do not believe this incarnation—this taking of the flesh—was some kind of vacation trip from which God returned to celestial places. It is a permanent commitment of the divine life to human flesh. The question we now confront as the nuclear arms race accelerates is what will happen to human flesh? Will it survive? Will it be incinerated? Peace in the nuclear age is now not only important but indispensable. It is a question of survival.

For me the key New Testament passage on peace comes near the end of the Gospel of Luke when Jesus weeps over the city and says, "Jerusalem, Jerusalem, if only you knew the things which *make* for peace. If only you recognized the *time* of your visitation." Peace, this passage says, is something to be *made*, and how it is made has to do with timing. In both regards, Jesus' next move shows us something about our responsibilities for peacemaking. After weeping over the city he dried his tears and immediately invaded the temple. Why?

We know that the temple in Jerusalem in Jesus' day was the place where all foreign currencies were deposited. It was the place one went to negotiate a loan, to cash the first-century equivalent of a check. It was the central headquarters of the local coalition which was cooperating with Roman imperial rule. It was also, of course, the religious center. It was the cathedral, the capitol, the bank, the insurance company, all rolled into one. It was this concentration of power that Jesus confronted, not with hatred, but with clarity.

I think this is what we are called on to do: to confront as unequivocably as possible those who are making the decisions to continue and escalate the arms race and to say to them just as clearly, *no*. We have had enough.

As of this writing, approximately fifty thousand nuclear weapons are in existence. About thirty thousand are in the hands of the United States and some twenty thousand are in the hands of the Soviet Union. A few other countries have a handful. That would seem to be sufficient. Yet we are told that the two super powers now plan to build ten thousand more nuclear weapons during the next decade. It will be a decade which, if anything, will be marked by more instability, more insecurity, more possibility for impulse and mistake. Yet, during that decade, the two super powers plan to add further weapons to their arsenals. This seems to be the moment Rosencrantz and Guildenstern were referring to: "Somewhere back there in the beginning, there must have been a point at which we could say, 'No.'"

There are many who think that after this next raising of the stakes of nuclear escalation, it will be less and less possible, and eventually impossible to turn back. There are stubborn technical reasons for this. The coming generation of nuclear weapons will be equipped with hair-trigger action and will be far more difficult to monitor. The newer weapons will allow insufficient time to ascertain exactly where a presumed attack is coming from or to find out for sure whether it is a real attack or not. Even more important, if no serious nuclear arms reduction begins soon among the superpowers it will become more and more difficult to persuade the present nonnuclear nations that they should not have their own arsenals.

* * * * *

With all this gnawing at my mind I returned from Japan in the late summer of 1978 determined to start doing something, anything, for nuclear disarmament. I called my old friend Beverly Woodward of the War Resisters League who told me she wanted my help in starting a peace education and action center in western Massachusetts. I told her I would be glad to, and a few months later we opened something we called the Traprock Peace Center, named for a type of stone found on the grounds.

Things moved very quickly. Within a few months the Traprock Center, along with the western Massachusetts office of the American Friends Service Committee, was in the thick of the first attempt to get a bilateral nuclear moratorium (later called a "freeze") on the ballot as a referendum question. We made the decision to try it in the early spring of 1980, quickly obtained the necessary signatures, and the question appeared on the ballot in three largely rural state senatorial districts in November 1980. It won in all three districts by an overall

majority of 59 percent. We were shocked and delighted but
that was only the beginning. Gradually at first, then in leaps
and bounds, the "freeze campaign" spread, first to the town
meetings of neighboring New Hampshire and Vermont, then
to other regions. I began devoting more and more of my time
to speaking for the freeze. I traveled to North Carolina,
Oregon, California, Pennsylvania. Randy Kehler, the young
man we hired to manage Traprock moved to St. Louis to head
a national "freeze" campaign. As I write this, in the early
summer of 1982, the idea of such a freeze has provided the
core around which a newly revitalized nationwide peace
movement has arisen. Over seven hundred thousand people
have just gathered in New York City for the largest peace
demonstration in human history. It seems that what happened
to me in Hiroshima has happened, in its own way, to millions of
other people. Somehow the taboo on speaking about nuclear
war has been broken. The paralysis and defeatism that once
kept people from acting has given way to a kind of confidence
that enough people acting in concert, can make a difference.

Peace pilgrims from all over the world came to New York for
the demonstration. But the most impressive delegation was a
group of survivors of the original American atomic bombing of
Japan. Just a week earlier I had met one of these survivors,
Mrs. Setsuko Thurlow, who is now living in Canada. Meeting
her made me think about how fast this has all happened. From
a handful of protesters a few years back, led by people who
were often viewed as extremists—like the Berrigan brothers
and the late Dorothy Day—the campaign against nuclear war
has grown into a mass popular movement. Mrs. Thurlow and I
talked about how it had happened, and why. Neither of us
could offer a plausible explanation. But we agreed that the
reservations we had both once harbored about the halfhearted
way the churches were particpating in the peace movement no
longer remained. Nearly half the American Catholic bishops
were now supporting a freeze. Billy Graham and the National
Council of Churches supported it. But even more importantly,
it had become a genuine grass-roots crusade. It was no longer

just church leaders, no longer something optional, no longer something on the edge.

When I told Mrs. Thurlow about my visit to Hiroshima I reminded her of what Einstein said about the atomic bomb, that it had changed everything, "except the way we think." She thought about that for a moment and then uttered something that, coming from a survivor of the first mushroom cloud, sounded more hopeful to me than anything I had heard for a long time. "That's true," she said, "but now maybe we are even beginning to change the way we think."

\* \* \* \* \*

In my own faith journey, which has carried me through Gdansk, Hiroshima, Utah, and western Massachusetts, I have decided my highest priority today is to try to prevent our species from joining the brontosaurus or the pterodactyl, perhaps taking our lovely, fragile planet along with it. I am now convinced that the worldwide church must become the advocate of all human life not as one among many possible emphases but as the central mission of its life. That time "somewhere near the beginning when we could have said no" is now.

I was locked up in Williamston, and I learned. I was stuck in Tehran, and I learned. I was paralyzed in Hiroshima, and I learned again. Must God always stop me in my tracks to make me listen? Maybe so.

# 14
# The Cloud of Witnesses

This is a thoroughly enjoyable section to write. Lots of people have helped me on my faith journey, many of them without even knowing it. In addition to the family figures I have already described there have been countless others. Here I am listing only ten (the roll could be much longer), recognizing as I write that to many of them this could come as a big surprise. Here goes (in order of my meeting them):

1. *Carroll Arnold,* pastor of the Malvern Baptist Church during my late high school and early college days. A navy veteran of World War II. Slightly cynical. A graduate of Eastern Baptist Seminary, theologically conservative but disdainful of fundamentalists. An intellectual who quoted Athanasius and Niebuhr in his sermons, to the puzzlement of most people in the congregation. A mystic who believed It was bigger than both of us. When I needed to believe the faith made sense and that I did not need to discard it to be an intellectual myself, he made sense.

2. *Edwin Aubrey,* Professor of Religious Thought, University of Pennsylvania, who died about 1952. A thoroughgoing

religious humanist and critic of neo-orthodoxy. I could never accept his theology, but he was an eloquent lecturer, a patient counselor and a brilliant historian of religion. Like Carroll Arnold he allowed me to see that it was not just intellectually mediocre people who were seriously religious. I also learned during my studying with Aubrey that he was a Welshman, that he came from a pietistic Baptist background. That created another link. Some day I want to write an appreciative article on him, especially since his old nemesis "Barthianism" has long since ceased to be the vanguard theology it was when he was entering the lists against it.

3. *Jane Doe,* a college sweetheart whom I never saw again after I graduated (she married someone else) and whose name need not be disclosed. Jane made it impossible for me ever to be a full-fledged male supremicist. I am glad it happened to me early on. She was, furthermore, a serious Christian and a crack tennis player. Also as smart as a whip, she argued with me about history and political theory and always won. She demolished my chauvinistic stereotypes and gave me a sense of what loving an equal might mean. She made Phi Beta Kappa and I did not.

4. *Earl Brill,* my roommate during my senior year at Penn. An intellectual and a Christian (albeit admittedly an Episcopalian), he was also a political activist and a lover of jazz and big band music. When he got terribly sick during that senior year and some people thought he would die, he remained amazingly cheerful while I fretted and worried. He was a bigger influence on me than he ever knew. Later on he became an Episcopal priest and now works at the College of Preachers in Washington, D.C. He also made Phi Beta Kappa and I. . . .

5. *Elizabeth Blakesley,* the director of the Oberlin College Student YWCA when I arrived at Oberlin just out of divinity school in 1955 to work as her colleague with the student YMCA. She was a mature and widely read woman with an infallible sense of humor and (I can see now) a lot of patience for self-congratulatory seminary graduates full of abstract ideas but without a clue about how one actually works with

students or with anyone else. Gently and jokingly she taught me, by example more than any other way, how not to lay my theological trip on so heavily, how to listen to people, how to swing with disappointment, how to work off frustration by smashing old crockery in the fireplace. She deserves a very large crown and multiple stars for putting up with such a talkative know-it-all pipsqueak. She also introduced me to feminist theology a decade or more before the term was invented.

6. *Nancy Cox*. She was an Oberlin College junior when I met her and later became my wife and the mother of our three children. She is the best friend I have ever had. When I first met her she was a Presbyterian flirting with becoming an Episcopalian. Later she became a Baptist (to keep the family pure) but has always retained a "high" sense of liturgy. She used to tell me the moment she liked best in church was when the service was all over and the acolytes put out the candles and the smoke from the extinguished wicks climbed to the ceiling. From her, more than anyone else, I have learned to pray. She writes prayers that are better by far than the ones in the prayerbook. An actress for the first fifteen years of our marriage, she taught me a lot about the reality of that realm of mystery that transcends concepts, but also about compassion for the underdog, patience, and how to listen to the music—the nuances and overtones—when a person speaks, instead of just to the words. She has been by far the most influential person in my faith journey.

7. *Martin Luther King, Jr.* I first met him when I was attending summer school in Nashville in 1956 and he gave a talk at Fisk University. We were the same age then, both twenty-seven, but he already had his doctorate (I had not yet begun to work on mine), and was leading the Montgomery bus boycott. Later I invited him to Oberlin and later still worked with him and with the Southern Christian Leadership Conference in a dozen odd campaigns and demonstrations. I consider his invitation to me to address the SCLC convention in Birmingham in 1966 the most distinguished honor I have ever received. King, like many of the other people who have

left their mark on my faith journey, did so because he was a preacher-scholar-prophet. He combined so well the things I aspired to be and do—and have never done as well as he. Also he always seemed to be a man who knew what God required of him at *this* particular time in history, not just in general. Nancy and I named our only son after King, and when King was killed in 1968 (while I was lecturing on "Theology of Hope" at Duke) I felt a loss that has never been repaired. That fact that he took time to encourage and appreciate me still seems astonishing, but it has helped keep me going for a long time.

8. *James Luther Adams,* now Professor Emeritus at Harvard, once my principal teacher and my Ph.D. adviser and mentor. Jim Adams is without a doubt the most brilliant teacher I have ever known. His choice, some years back, was to devote his energy to teaching and guiding his students even if that decision would cut into his scholarly output. A legendary figure (people still say he only sleeps four hours a night), a walking bibliography in four languages, a spirited and dramatic lecturer, he is a sort of identity model for me as a university professor, although an extremely hard act to follow. Perhaps the most remarkable thing of all about JLA is that although he has supervised the doctoral research of dozens of people now teaching theology, ethics, religion and society, and related fields, there is absolutely no "Adams school." His students pursue disparate interests and differ widely from one another in theological and political opinion. Adams once asked me to read an article in Dutch for a seminar the following week, believing—I assume—that any intelligent person who knew a little German and could locate a Dutch-English dictionary should be able to read such an article. It was the kind of unintended compliment he handed out all the time and for which I will always be grateful.

9. *Bruno Schotstädt,* pastor in the Lutheran Church in Berlin, leader of the Gossner Mission in East Berlin where I served as an Ecumenical Fraternal Worker in 1962-63. Bruno, a loyal citizen of East Germany, the founder of the German equivalent of the French "worker priest" movement and my

immediate chief during my formative year in Berlin, is the person mainly responsible for challenging the unexamined "Western" and "bourgeois" assumptions in my faith and my theology. He did so not by being balanced but by being outrageously one-sided on occasion. Always good-humored even when needling me, he helped me see the reality of Dietrich Bonhoeffer's "this worldly" Christianity as I worked in the city where Bonhoeffer had taught and preached and struggled and died. Bruno even looked a little like Bonhoeffer (plump and Prussian, a bit jowly) and became for me a kind of reincarnation of that martyred rebel against Hitler.

10. *Don Sergio Mendez Arceo,* Roman Catholic bishop of Cuernevaca, Mexico, and unofficial prelate of the whole "Catholic left" in Latin America. I first met this hulking, bald scholar-priest when, at the invitation of Ivan Illich, the bishop and I taught a seminar together on "Liturgy in the Secular City" at the Center for Intercultural Documentation in Cuernavaca during the summer of 1968. Mendez Arceo is the originator of the popular "Mariachi Mass" celebrated every Sunday in the cathedral there. Since our seminar I have never missed a chance to visit or talk with him. Most recently we worked together on a series of public hearings which he helped organize in Mexico City on the violation of El Salvadorean human rights. Don Sergio represents many things for me. He stands for the nearly miraculous rebirth of Christianity among the Latin American poor, a phenomenon hardly anyone could have foreseen three decades ago. He also embodies the possibility of the Christian struggle for liberation not on the periphery of the church but at its center. He is after all a bishop and not a "marginado." Whenever I get unusually discouraged about the institutional church and begin to think the only way to preserve the gospel from corruption is to cut loose from it, I think of Don Sergio, usually in full liturgical dress including cope and mitre. Then I remember that more things are possible within the church than the evidence sometimes suggests. He not only symbolizes the presence of the church in the liberation process, he is one of the people who put it there.

# 15
# Just as I Am

Readers who grew up as I did in an evangelical Baptist church will not need to have the title of this book explained to them. It is the name of the hymn that is often sung during revival services, after the sermon, when a life without God and hell's terrors have just been vividly painted and the doors are opened to accept Christ and be saved. The "invitation" is given. And now "with every head bowed and every eye closed" the preacher or the visiting evangelist urges those in the congregation who have not yet made their decision for Christ to come forward. The organ or piano plays "Just as I Am." The choir, often with the congregation humming along, sings too . . . "without one plea,/But that thy blood was shed for me."

Though the words may sound lachrymose to many, for me they still convey a sense of comfort and assurance. Was I really acceptable to God "just as I am"? Was it really true that I needed no improvements, no alterations, that I could enter the presence of the Most High, the terrifying *mysterium tremendum* (as I later learned to say) *just* as I am? If true, that was very good news to an adolescent who was always being reminded—or so it

151

seemed to me—of my shortcomings and defects. I was never good at football or basketball. Someone else played the saxophone sweeter than I did. Most of the girls seemed to prefer other guys for dates. Although I did fairly well in my classes there was always someone, usually one of the girls, who got a higher score on the exam. Both my parents seemed to love me unconditionally but, like all kids, I sensed behind their expressions of affection a lot of hopes and expectations I was not sure I could live up to.

But God accepted me just as I am?

That was not judgment but good news. Years later, when I read Paul Tillich's famous sermon entitled "You Are Accepted," I knew exactly what it meant, and I could hear the melody of the old hymn still humming on in the back of my mind.

Now the time has come to close this book about my faith journey and, once again, the perfectionist pressures instilled in me by a productivity-driven culture war within me against the assurance that I am accepted "just as I am" and that this book will have to be ended "just as it is."

Ending a book about my faith journey is no easier than beginning it. The book must end. The journey lurches on. My keenest sensation as I begin this final chapter is that so much has been left out. Teaching is my main work. Yet, except for casual references here and there I have written hardly anything about my students and colleagues at the various institutions where I have taught and, while teaching, have learned; yet they have all been companions of the road. I have to ask myself what this seemingly strange oversight signifies. Why has it not occurred to me to devote more pages to the role my teaching (and writing) have played in my faith journey? I think I know the answer.

I have never been what some people call a "career-oriented" person. My father, remember, lost his little company before it gave him much satisfaction and was, in any case, never all that enthusiastic about it. Like my grandmother Maude he had had some political aspirations but, unlike her, his never came to much. Also he sometimes preferred racing sheets to account ledgers and poker chips to business memos. I may have learned from him that career is not necessarily where the action is.

The matrix of my faith journey has not been my work but my personal ties on the one hand and my extra-curricular political, ecumenical and peace work on the other. In my "career" I have been a bit lethargic, staying at the same institution for nearly two decades (and never even becoming a dean!). I have been more emotionally involved in family, church, and "causes" than in my career. I do not belong to any professional associations and I do not take part in the theology "guild."

Still, the places I have worked have influenced me more than this book would indicate. I have been at Harvard University— in and out, boy and man—since the fall of 1958. At this writing that amounts to twenty-four years, a long time to be part of any institution. When I confess to people that I still feel a little like a stranger at Harvard, they invariably chuckle. A tenured professor, around the Yard for nearly a quarter of a century? What would it take to feel at home?

Part of the problem undoubtedly is that as an overly cerebral high school kid I always held Harvard in awe. The books I read about the people I admired always seemed to paint it as the apex of intellectual achievement. I wanted to go to Harvard but I never applied because my family thought I should go to Penn. It was closer to home. And cheaper. I did go to Penn and I have never been sorry. I got what I consider to be a superb undergraduate education, majored in European history, wrote my honors thesis on the Russian Revolution and nearly stayed on to pursue doctoral work in history. But I decided to go to divinity school during my senior year in college and, since Harvard's school of theology was at that time virtually unknown, I went to Yale. It was only when I decided to get a Ph.D. that I eventually got to Harvard.

All through my years of doctoral study at Harvard I was also teaching at Andover-Newton Theological School, so I was never part of the Harvard "scene," did not reside in one of the river houses, write for *The Crimson* or the *Lampoon,* try out for one of the notorious clubs, or participate in student political life. This has made a difference. I have discovered that at Harvard no matter how many doctorates one holds from any of the graduate schools, the soul of the university is still Harvard College, and unless you went there, you will always be something of an outsider. After years of puzzling over this curious blood bond created by the old school tie, I have now reconciled myself to it. With a doctorate, a crimson robe, and an endowed chair I am still something of a wayfarer at America's oldest university. I am ineligible for membership in the inner club.

Teaching at Harvard is a taxing joy. I often become angry and lose patience with the endless demands of the students. But when I hear colleagues from other colleges talk about how hard it is to "motivate" their students, I just cannot imagine what they are talking about. Whatever else you have to do to Harvard students, you do not have to motivate them. They are eager, critical, sometimes skeptical, not always terribly appreciative, incessantly stimulating. By now I have taught students from virtually every division of the university. This includes the law school, school of education, schools of medicine and public health, and the school of design. I enjoy them all, but perhaps the ones—outside the divinity school—I like the most are the enthusiastic adult learners who come into my classes from Harvard's ambitious continuing education division. Insurance agents, taxi drivers, legal secretaries, homemakers, business executives, retired persons—they are the kind of people who work hard at another job (except for the retired ones) and then come to classes. To accommodate them I even scheduled one of my courses for later afternoon so they could come after work.

I consider myself to be an original if not very thorough scholar, rather imaginative in sensing connections and creating syntheses. Not too careful of details. Terrible at footnotes. But I consider myself to be an excellent teacher. In seminars I like to draw people out and push them into discussions with one another. I try to take seriously even the most uninformed contribution and I welcome what might appear to be stupid questions (there are not many) since I have come to believe what an older professor told me years ago when I started teaching: good students may seem to ask silly questions, but bad students ask no questions at all. As a lecturer, I draw heavily on my experience both as a preacher and a debater on the Penn team. I enjoy lecturing, and student evaluations usually say I do it well, with an occasional complaint that I am not as well organized as I might be and that I often go too fast. In any case, I love to teach, and during those occasional years when I have had a semester leave for research and writing I have missed it desperately.

As I reach the middle-fifties years in my journey I sense a subtle change in my attitude toward my students. Years ago I often felt intimidated by them, afraid they knew more than I did. Then I began to think of teaching as an exchange: I knew some things they did not and vice versa. I still feel that way in some measure, but I have also begun to realize that at my age I *do* have some knowledge and experience they do not (most of them at least) and that they deserve to draw on some of the wisdom and lore the years have given me. I have also begun to take more personal pleasure in the accomplishments of my students. I find myself boasting about the ones who have made good or done significant things, much as a parent cannot help feeling proud of his or her children. I find that this in turn helps me feel a little more supportive of those students who are at earlier stages where they have not been able to accomplish much yet. Now I even enjoy seeing them take the little steps that will get them there someday—a term paper better written than the last one, a new-found enthusiasm for an idea. Developmental psychologists like Erik Erikson tell us that at my stage in life the battle we fight is between generativity and stagnation. I hope I can avoid stagnation. And my students now provide my best shot at generativity.

Writing books is also, I suppose, a "generating" task. In that area, my dilemma is that of having "peaked" too early. My first book, *The Secular City,* became an international best seller and was eventually translated into eleven languages. I wrote it when I was thirty-four. After that I went through an immense "second book crisis," something I had heard other writers complain about. The crisis happens when you sit down to scribble and suddenly realize that hundreds of thousands of people may ponder the next word you inscribe. It is enough to paralyze anyone's fingers. I scuffled with that freeze for a few years but eventually wrote *The Feast of Fools* which still remains my own favorite. It is the "one book" I recommend to people who ask me at parties which *one* of my books they should crack. Of my other books I am probably least pleased with *The Seduction of the Spirit* which I think has the best first chapter of anything I have ever written (about my boyhood in Malvern, Pennsylvania, the churches there and my baptism), but goes downhill after that. I enjoyed doing the research for *Turning East* which involved nosing around various Asian-inspired religious movements and teaching at the Tibetan-Buddhist-led Naropa Institute in Boulder, Colorado. But it was something of a detour from my continuing theological interests. My forthcoming book, tentatively entitled *After the Secular City,* will probably occupy my attention for the next two years. It will be an effort to look at the issues I dealt with in *The Secular City*—like urbanization, secularization, and the relation of religion to the modern world—and assess what has happened and where to go from here. The fact that such a book will have to deal with such global issues intimidates me now more than it did a decade and a half ago. Aging and constant exposure to the timid atmosphere of academia have a way of making anyone more cautious about risking any kind of generalization, and this leads either to narrower specialization or to silence. But I do not want to settle for either.

There are other places I have taught that have also made their mark on me.

There was Oberlin College where I began my "career" as a college chaplain and drank up the lively tradition of radical congregational abolitionism, feminism and peacemaking that still enlivens that campus. There was Andover Newton Theological School where I first started teaching theology mainly to pay my way through graduate school and discovered to my surprise just how much I liked to do it. There was the Baptist Seminary of Mexico where during two unforgettable semesters I taught students who were not learning to preach in suburban churches but to face the life-and-death pressures of Nicaragua and El Salvador. It was also at that seminary that I imbibed the intellectual challenge and spiritual verve of Latin American theology. There was the Naropa Institute in Boulder, Colorado, which I have described at some length in *Turning East* where I had to grapple with the challenge of the Buddhist *dharma* to my mind and my soul. To tell what I learned at any or all of them would require another volume.

I have also of course left out much that is too intimate, too sensitive, too revealing of other people to be included in a book. A pity, since all of us are probably shaped most in our faith journeys precisely by the things that are the most awkward to disclose, the kind of material that belongs in archives, to be opened years after the deaths of all the principals. No hint here that I have lived some elaborate secret life that will only come to light after my own demise: I only want to underline what any reader who is sensitive to the vital ingredients of his or her own faith journey already knows, that often what is most impossible to describe is what has been most important.

As I reread the pages I have written here in an effort to bring them to a close what impresses me most of all is that my faith journey has been inextricably bound up with passing the faith on: not just my passing it on to others, but the others who passed it on to me. The conversations I have mentioned here, between myself and my father and between my son and myself are symbolic of the whole journey. Somehow my son sensed, while I was telling stories of the sixties, that he would one day be telling his stories too. "I pass on to you what was passed on to me." He was also aware that unless we turn back from the nuclear brink he will *not* be telling stories to his children as I told mine to him.

Passing it on makes the difference. The miracle for me is not that some of our children, sensing the nuclear menace we have thrust upon them, wander off into hedonism and confusion. The miracle is that many of them do their algebra, keep their heads on, and make their way into adulthood with a degree of serenity and poise. Are they repressing a mountainous glob of fatalism, not allowing themselves to think about it when they sit down to work out their problem sets, lest the whole enterprise appear so useless they could not turn the next page? Maybe. But I believe our stories have reached deeper into them than we allow ourselves to think. They have a faith which goes beyond the symbols and creeds. The stories we tell them convey the sense that there is something that makes living worthwhile even when the experts say there is no point, since nuclear war has become statistically more probable with every passing day. My faith has been fed by the refusal of the young people who came into the world after Hiroshima to resign or to become cynical voluptuaries. They are the first generation to approach maturity knowing that the whole thing could be over in an instant: *kapow*. All things considered, they are doing pretty well. They want, someday, to tell their stories too.

Biblical faith is a generational phenomenon. It comes alive as it is lived out and passed on. My own faith grows and deepens—if and when it does—mostly when I act on it and when I try to give it to someone else, usually my children but also to my students. What is real and what is ersatz, what I believe and what I think I believe (or would like to believe), sort themselves out when I face that generational bridge-and-barrier, that awful obligation we have to help the next cadre of human beings make sense out of the senseless. This taxing test has taught me that faith is not just something Abraham, Isaac, and Jacob shared (as did Sarah, Rebekah, and Rachel) but something which *came into being as it was passed along.* My tongue-tied efforts to link, in these pages, the eighteenth-century Quakers with the present, myself with my readers, the sixties with the eighties, is the stuff of which faith and faith journeying are made. This book has made me, as it were, come clean. It has become part of a passing on that goes back to the Welsh Quakers who built the Goshen Meeting House, to Maude's campaign buttons, to my father's lost battle to do the work he wanted to do in a world that made it impossible. Writing these pages has made me look honestly at what I feel today about those marches and demonstrations of the sixties and about raising our paleskin family in blacktown. It has forced me to remember the hard chair and the humorless faces of the interrogation room at Checkpoint Charlie and what I said and would like to have said at the questioning. It has brought back the nauseating terror I tasted in Teheran and the watery wobbling of my knees in Hiroshima. It has allowed me to blurt out the fascination I have always fostered, from the outside, for the hoary old church of Rome, and to put down in black-and-white the affection-mixed-with-frustration I cherish for the precarious little congregation that is my home church. What it all adds up to is that my faith seems to be more connectional than creedal, more a matter of where I have come from and where I am heading—and who is doing it with me—than a registering of convictions attained or beliefs held.

Some contemporary philosophers believe that human beings think by putting things in words, that if we believe we have an idea but cannot express it, we do not really have it yet. This may not be true for other people, but it is true for me. I often find myself saying something, or writing something, I had just not thought of before I expressed it. Only when it comes to speech—silent, written, or spoken—does a thought attain any reality for me. Consequently this rambling and disjointed account has not just been a description of my faith journey or a resumé of the process of passing it on. It has been a part of the journey and of the passing it on. My fondest hope is that those who have stayed with me this far have also done some journeying and some passing it on while they have been reading. And as I end I take some satisfaction in knowing that just as the journey began long before I appeared, it will continue after I am gone.